Women Living in
Alignment

Stories of Embracing
the Heart, Soul, and Energy as One

Compiled By
Sue Urda
Kathy Fyler

Powerful You!
PUBLISHING
Sharing Wisdom ~ Shining Light

Women Living In Alignment
Stories of Embracing the Heart, Soul, and Energy as One

Copyright © 2022

Published by: Powerful You! Inc. USA
powerfulyoupublishing.com

Library of Congress Control Number: 2022916336

Sue Urda and Kathy Fyler – First Edition

ISBN: 978-1-959348-00-9

First Edition November 2022

Self-Help

Dedication

*This book is dedicated to those
who wish to connect
with their inner knowing
and align their life
to live in a space of grace and ease.*

Table of Contents

Table of Contents

Foreword

I am so honored to be asked to write the foreword of this important book because to me everything hinges on our alignment. It is fundamental to our happiness, fulfillment, well-being, and success. It invites more ease, joy, and pleasure into our life. Alignment is a sacred connection with ourselves that allows us to feel grounded, safe, supported, nurtured, and deeply nourished from within.

When we are in alignment we live from a place of truth, authenticity, transparency, and integrity. We are able to stay centered and calm. We radiate light and love, and we are in a space of flow where everything falls into place as we vibrate at the exact frequency of the happiness, love, growth, contribution, and money that we desire.

There is a huge shift happening on the planet right now. We are moving from the paradigm of merely surviving to thriving, by coming back into alignment with our true selves. To facilitate this, we are being called to release all that no longer serves us. Anything that is inauthentic can no longer survive. False identities and beliefs are being exposed, dismantled, and stripped away. We have an intolerance for lower vibrational things reflected in conversations, attitudes, societal structures and more.

When we are out of alignment, we feel disconnected, discouraged, and stressed. We find ourselves rushing onto the next 'to-do' on our list. We push and force to try to make things happen, but not really getting anywhere. When we aren't in alignment, feeling exhausted, overwhelmed, and frazzled is the norm. Our parasympathetic nervous system is screaming for us to slow down; trying to get our attention.

We all have a unique pain point in our body that alerts us when we have come out of alignment. We may quickly get a stomachache or a headache or heart palpitations to let us know what is derailing us so we can get back on track. It's incredibly important that we don't ignore these cues as our alignment is integral to our lives working for us, as is deeply nourishing ourselves.

I've noticed a common thread with the thousands of people I have worked with over the years—as I bring an awareness that taking time for themselves and filling their cup first is essential and necessary to be in alignment; it is often met with resistance and incites feelings of selfishness, guilt, and shame because we, as women in particular, have been taught that everyone and everything else comes first—which couldn't be further from the truth. We must fill ourselves first to be in alignment with our soul and unlock our wildest dreams.

Helping people live a thriving, rich, freedom-filled life on purpose and in alignment with their soul is the heart of my business. I had the pleasure of working with Sue and Kathy years ago when they published my first story. At that time, their integrity and authenticity spoke deeply to my soul, and still does to this day. When something resonates with you, you know it and it takes a huge amount of bravery and courage to act on that, especially when so many people are disconnected and out of touch with their true selves.

Reading these heartfelt, inspiring stories these brave souls have so boldly shared will help you to heal, awaken, and inspire your own confidence and inner alignment—and truly, that's when the real magic shows up.

Warmly,
Lisa Stamper
Intuitive Life and Business Coach
Spiritual Channel and Healer

Introduction

Storytelling is and art and a calling.
It is a gift, a contribution, a love letter to the world.
Storytelling is beneficial for the reader ~
and perhaps even more for the author.

Most authors featured in this book came forth already open and willing to go to the depths of their personal journeys. They knew their stories could change the hearts, minds, and even the lives of readers. Others came to their stories 'kicking and screaming"—even though it was they who made the choice to open their hearts. Interestingly, those who fought themselves the hardest along the way to painstakingly bare their souls are now content in the knowledge that they stepped forward from their inner self and unleashed their heart for the higher good, knowing that if one soul is touched the fear and deep inner work of writing is well worth it.

The simple act of stepping into the work and allowing oneself to be vulnerable provides healing for the heart and soul.

And so, herein lie the hearts, souls, and energy of 20 incredible women. Some of them had no idea they were writers until the title of this book and the opportunity to collaborate called to them. They were drawn by some compelling force to open to the truth of themselves. Now, on the other side of the writing process, they will tell you that they have put forth not only their hearts and souls, they also reveal the essence of some very important aspects of their lives.

When you are called to share your story, there's nothing that will stop you; not fear, not angst, not lack of confidence, not the monkey mind, and certainly not the voice of anyone else. The call, the pull, is so great it must be answered. It's as if the choice is not really yours…although of course, the calling is your own inner voice, and it must be affirmatively answered.

In talking with each of the authors, we know that the overwhelming reason and decision to write their story was to help someone else who is searching for answers, someone who needs encouragement and a light shone on the path before them. Many write of the synchronicity of their transformation or the happy story of how things work out beautifully no matter the starting point. Others share secrets that they have guarded for many years and, for the first time, emerge from their silence because of the opening, opportunity, and healing that comes along with it. No matter their reason, they each decided the time to share her story is now.

What they all discovered is that an energetic transformation occurs when one puts pen to paper (or fingers to the keypad) with the intent to reveal her truth. As you read each story in this book, you will find yourself feeling the very core of the emotion of each author, whether she is speaking of creating or expanding a business, healing from some sort of tragedy, trauma, or abuse in her life, opening to her inborn gifts and talents, or she is still finding her way to living in alignment.

Each transformation is unique and holds its own gifts.

Alignment. If you are drawn to the title of this book, you are undoubtedly on your own journey of awakening to a more conscious way of being. You are ready to step more fully into your power and align with it—in fact, by picking up this book, you're already doing it. You have already leapt ahead towards your destination and, as you flip through the pages and read the stories, you will catapult yourself even further along this path. Why? Because we are all connected, and your desire and willingness cannot help but move you forward. The only question is, *will you go forth with ease?*

Are you ready to live in alignment,
embracing your heart, soul, and energy as one?
We believe you are, and these stories will assist you.

Our wish for you is that you commit to yourself to be aware of your calling, your purpose, your joy. Delve into your heart, listen to your inner voice, answer the call of your soul's purpose—however great or quiet, wherever it shows up, and whatever or whoever is the bearer. Be faithful to your desire to live in alignment with your heart space. As you do this, you will find your life to be more filled with love, more guided by Spirit, and more consciously aligned with your own heart, soul, and energy.

With deep gratitude and love,
Sue Urda & Kathy Fyler

CHAPTER 1

Nice to Meet Me

Dr. Diana Salazar

We all do it: start the day by brushing our teeth and looking in the mirror. But how we speak to ourselves in that quick glance matters. It took a while to see my reflection as a woman, a doctor, and a person who confidently speaks to herself with kindness and love.

This journey required me to give up being "the baby." The princess identity I so lovingly held as the youngest in my family. This journey required me to see myself as smart, knowledgeable, and strong so I could lead my bad ass, equally strong patients to their health goals. This journey to inner confidence also required the loss of love and the destruction of my job. Lastly, embracing my true energetic self required me to be alone so I could step into the parts of me that I'd shut off. None of these revelations were easy or fun. I quickly learned they're called "growing pains" for a reason. New awareness costs rejection of old views and walking away from how life was. All of these were important to my alignment.

Giving up "The Princess"

In chiropractic school I began meditating, mostly out of the need to calm my anxiety. The practice helped me through emotional moments; stress before big tests; or nights I couldn't sleep because I felt anxious about the tiniest things that felt heavy on my heart. When in deep meditation there was (and still is) one place I always ended up: a white, heaven-like room. I'd walk down to a bench—the kind Forrest Gump would have a deep conversation on—in the middle of the wide open, white, infinite space. Each time, there would be a woman already sitting on the left side of the bench. As I sat down next to her, I noticed that she looked like me, but older. Her skin sparkled, her smile illuminated the space, her energy was calm and confident.

My twenty-something-year-old self went to this room in agony, searching for comfort and a path that makes sense. And every time, this future Me ended the conversation, and my worries, with the same phrase: "Don't worry. You'll get to me. Keep going. You'll get to me!"

Her power is what truly made me pack my clothes, stay persistent against the frustrations of getting licensed in a tough state like New York, and leave my beautiful life in California.

In L.A., I was comfortable and happy. I had my support system with friends and a large loving family. I had a sunny, perfect temperature with little traffic kind of life. I was grateful for it all. Yet I knew in my heart that there was no way I would be able to get to that version of Me by living a life that made everyone else happy. I didn't know what was waiting for me in New York City. All I knew was "She" was the person I needed to become.

I believe you live in alignment when you work towards the dreams that don't leave you. The dreams that persist and call you over and over again, relentlessly, until you answer. Making you rise up and do the work. For me, that meant taking steps towards the dream of fully embracing myself. It meant surrounding myself with the community that would open my mind.

Intuition is Not a Bad Word

I remember being really energetically intuitive at a young age. My mother has fibromyalgia and, as the youngest of five, I would be the one to give her a massage when she needed it. There I was, ten years old, and saying, "I know, Mom, that you have pain in your wrist, but I think it's coming from your elbow." I was known as her "little doctor"; "healing hands"; and the "Doogie Howser" of the Salazar house. Then, as a teenager, my energetic intuition became confusing because it seemed to conflict with my religious background. I saw it as a sensitivity I neither wanted nor understood so I decided to shut it out. I declared out loud, "I don't want this anymore," then I went to bed and didn't give it another thought... until chiropractic school.

While there, I had a roommate who did Reiki and friends who were spiritually awake and spoke the language of intuition. Very slowly, the walls around that part of myself started to come down. I began scrubbing away the words I had marked against myself that took away a huge portion of what makes me fully Me. I knew that the "future me" owned that energetic side. I could tell by the way she responded to my questions of confusion and need for support. She wasn't afraid.

Leaving Los Angeles would be my opportunity to completely embrace and reinvent myself, like a kid at a new school. I would no longer be a sister, daughter, friend, or partner first. I would just be me. Alone to be bored and creative. Quiet so I could hear my voice speak in an apartment where only I had the key.

I learned how to say, "Hi, I'm Dr. Diana Salazar. I mix energetic work and Chiropractic"—such a simple statement that took seven years to embody.

This took unlearning being a princess and treating myself like a queen. It took only buying essential groceries that I could hold on the five-block walk to my apartment. It took pushing through the wind and snow slapping me across the face until finding refuge in a subway station. It took losing my job during the pandemic, bringing on a deep depression that made it hard to look at myself in the mirror. It took heartbreaks that brought so much darkness that I prayed to God, the Universe, and the California waves to remind me who I was. It took patients feeling better and telling me that I helped them. Most importantly, it took me piecing myself together and learning what I wanted to keep in my story.

Through it all, I kept meditating. Going back to that same white room in my mind. Pushing my comfort levels and staying the path, even if I felt like I was going against the grain of sanity. I couldn't explain why I stayed in the epicenter of the pandemic rather than returning to my sunny life. To endure the eerie moments of being one of five people on a train during a time of increased violence in the city—a Gotham without a caped crusader.

The Way to Gain is to Lose

It wasn't until I'd lost my job that I realized how low my self-esteem really was. My life revolved around helping other people feel better. It had become my validation, giving me a boost and confirming I was smart enough for people to listen to me. Now, with no job and no significant other, I was left only with my thoughts. I also noticed that when in social settings my inner voice would ramble on about how I wasn't good enough, not smart enough, not financially savvy enough, and not political enough. My strengths and calling were put on hold. Before 2020, I thought I was okay—living in alignment and very confident. And at times, I was, but true inner confidence is unshakeable.

Growth has ups, downs, and flat planes. When your best relationship is with yourself, everything changes. Challenging moments are only that, no longer attached with your self-worth. The moments of excitement are filled with gratitude instead of validation. The story you tell yourself about what others think about you begins to fade away. It no longer matters, because you love who you are.

Through it all, I stayed the course, all for "her". I was thirty-three, the city was coming back, and so was my sense of self. Much had happened and I had changed. I had made the decision to stay in New York and after work began writing and producing music, a dream I never thought could come true. I had a new appreciation for each patient as they had made the same eerie trip into the office. I came out of my deep depression and began truly loving myself.

I went back to my meditation. The room was the same: white, bright, and calming with a bench in the center of it. But this time, for the first time, she was not sitting waiting for me. I sat down and turned, where she usually was, and saw a large mirror. With a confused expression on my face, I moved my head left and right to verify it is indeed my reflection. Immediately the mirror leaves and someone takes its place on the bench. It's me, exactly as I am now. No more illuminated face, not a different age. No longer a "Her" but, "Me," saying, "You got to me!" I immediately cry tears of celebration in my mind and physically. A journey that had felt heavy and hard immediately made sense. All of it was worth it. Through the pain and darkness, I learned to shine my light so I could hold my patients' pain with compassion and created an energetic practice in alignment with my passions and possibilities.

Leading Leaders

The beauty of Manhattan is that it makes you rise to the occasion or it kicks you out. Having patients who are no nonsense creatives, bad asses, and hustlers in their fields means you need to lead the leaders. Regardless of who you are and what you do, everyone just wants to feel comforted and that they are walking confidently in the direction of their goals. There is something heavenly in creating a space that lets people relax and be present. In order to lead, you need to have confidence.

Mine grew in steps and, sometimes, from the outside in. I made sure to start the day wearing something that made me feel powerful. Dressing for success with my favorite earrings, great shoes, or an outfit that made me smile. Consciously reducing filler words, only speaking with intention and listening more so that others feel heard. As someone who is growth-driven, I didn't realize that I was being mean to myself when en route to a goal. I felt frustrated, disappointed, and impatient that I hadn't yet arrived. I was missing the joy in the journey. Being goal-oriented doesn't mean beating myself up for not being at the destination. I learned to remember the distance I had made so far to fuel me the rest of the way.

Alignment is fluid. It can be a specific unchanging destination and a moment later, it can change into something larger than what you could have ever imagined. Kobe Bryant has been one of my greatest teachers of this. I had the honor of being in the crowd at his retirement ceremony—a memory that is woven into my heart. As he stood at the center of the court speaking to his daughters, the crowd faded away, and he was no longer an icon, just a father speaking to his kids. He told them, "Those times when you don't feel like working. You're too tired. You don't want to push yourself, but you do it anyway. That is actually the dream."

Being in alignment is doing the work—not being perfect and always getting it right, but doing little things so you can rest your head at the end of the day knowing you are walking toward it. Sometimes to learn what being in alignment is you have to know what it's like to be out of it. Contrast gives clarity. You have to know what a "No" feels like in your body, mind, and spirit to know what "Yes" is. This can mean making choices that later on can feel like mistakes. Perfectionism is the way to stagnation. Going for it, unafraid to make mistakes, learning how to humbly forgive myself was the greatest way I was able to have compassion for others. Feeling what it's like to be out of alignment gave me the opportunity to learn to make choices that are better for my highest self.

Being in alignment is not sunshine and rainbows but it is the opportunity to authentically shine in the way only you can. It's been my greatest joy to hold space for people's healing and my own. We are layer upon layer of muscle, bone, ligaments, nerves, arteries, and energy, and just like hitting your elbow creates a level of discomfort, so does emotional stress. As an energetic healer, I hold space to help my patients release grief, sadness, and work through stress so they can decrease the residue on their bodies. I assist people to get over a break-up and embrace change—both situations I can relate to. Decreasing emotional heaviness in the body makes people stand taller and stronger. They walk and move differently when their body is in better physical alignment. It's an inner power and confidence that grows over time as we move towards our goals.

The key is to stop, adapt, and listen to your internal voice. Savor the moments that bring you joy and keep moving forward towards your own shiny version of you.

What does that person look like? What makes them smile? How strong are they and how can you work towards that? There will be questions that you know the answer to, and when you don't that's also an answer. Curiosity and courage allow your own magic to occur. Enjoy the ride, smile at your brilliant self in the mirror and say it's...Nice to Meet Me.

ABOUT THE AUTHOR: Dr. Diana Salazar is an Energetic Chiropractor blending gentle adjustments, postural training, and intuitive healing. She is passionate about helping people feel powerful, stable, and educated so they can proactively take care of their bodies for their future. Born and raised in Los Angeles, in 2017 Dr. Diana graduated with her Doctorate in Chiropractic from Southern California University of Health Sciences (SCUHS). She is licensed in New York State, and lives and practices in Manhattan. Much of her intuition, warmth, and resilience comes from her Ecuadorian roots. Dr. Diana is a lover of leather jackets, fall weather, and palm trees.

Dr. Diana Salazar
chirointhecity.com
Instagram: @chirointhecity

CHAPTER 2

Stubborn is Good, but Listen!

Dr. Donna W. Woo

"Mama, please tell me again!" I beg. I need her to repeat the story, to make sure I have all the details, before it's too late.

She is on an oxygen machine, barely able to breathe, but she manages to say, "The first time the doctor said yes, then changed his mind and said no. The second time I was in the waiting room and that doctor *died*. The third time, another doctor said yes, but then it was too late because I was too far along."

"Really? The doctor *died* while *you* were *waiting* in the waiting room?" I ask, though I've heard it before. What are the chances of that happening?!

The story is important because it could explain why I was here, despite the times I had wished I wasn't or did not know my purpose. It could also explain why Mom often called me stubborn.

For most of my life, I thought stubborn was a negative trait. This caused self-doubt, insecurity, feeling bad about who I am, and sadness because I craved approval, especially from my family. I have since learned that being stubborn can be positive, that it means persistence or living in alignment with my values. However, as I wrote in the book, *Women Living on Purpose: Real Stories of Women Living with Passion, Intention, and Vision,* living in alignment is not always a straight line.

Not only did it take me over twelve years to become a chiropractic physician, but it has taken me decades to reclaim my power and happiness by speaking up, setting boundaries, and building a strong relationship with *myself*. When I do these things for myself, I can actually help others. Being at peace with myself contributes to peace in the world.

Remembering To Listen

I have always felt guided by "angels," like someone/something/ Universe was always watching over me. So I know that when things do not turn out the way I want them to, I must set aside my "positive stubbornness." Instead of getting upset or frustrated or feeling hopeless, I need to ask, "What lesson am I supposed to be learning from this?"

For instance, I would have liked to write this chapter about how my husband had finally stopped gaslighting, sneaking, and drinking too much for good, so I could report to you that I had a success story. I would have liked to say that my stubbornness and persistence for living in alignment with my values, speaking up, setting boundaries, and learning to love myself finally paid off one hundred percent. I would have reported I was totally living in alignment with being "Healthy, Wealthy, and Married"—one of the mottos my husband and I have.

I would also report my "1+1=1"—another motto of ours—was foolproof. This is not a "you complete me scenario." It means our relationship is only as strong as each of us individually. (We have since added 1+1+1=1 for our new puppy!)

Well, Universe had other plans again.

Instead of focusing on how perfect life can be and how happy we can be once our goals are achieved, Universe reminded me about progress over perfection and how we can be happy NOW and enjoy each day as best we can, not just when things are perfect. Thus, I am not writing a fairytale, but about the roller coaster of life, and how we can always reclaim our power and happiness, no matter the ups and downs. Also, roller coasters can even be fun—that is why they are at amusement parks—so learn to enjoy the ride!

Speaking Up Respectfully

Although roller coasters can be fun, being on one for too long can get exhausting. Staying in alignment means speaking up when it is time to take a pause.

I used to be so afraid to speak up for several reasons, including not wanting to hurt someone's feelings; not being liked; not wanting to be judged; not wanting to be annoying or rude; not feeling safe; having shame; wanting to be respectful; or wanting to keep the peace.

For example, I remember being with my coaches at a restaurant. I was cold but did not say anything because I did not want to be annoying or seem demanding or disagreeable. One of the coaches noticed I was shivering and asked me if I was cold. I said I was, and he asked if I would like to sit somewhere warmer! I was amazed that I could actually say how I felt and it was okay and others were willing to help me.

Sometimes, however, speaking up may not seem so simple. I had been so afraid to speak up publicly about my husband's alcohol use. I was not only protecting him, but myself. I have had so much shame around it because it is not in alignment with my values. I also am not proud of some of my own behavior, including screaming from frustration, on the worst nights. I believe in preventing illness and being in control of my own behavior. Besides worrying about his health, I believed his drinking was a reflection on me. I was teaching thousands of patients to be healthy, yet I was unable to help the one I loved the most. Then my own health was affected by the stress.

However, because of my stubbornness (a.k.a. persistence/living in alignment) and because I consistently spoke up, my husband has become aware of his drinking habits and cut down drastically. In fact, he lost so much weight this year that a woman approached me at the gym and asked if I had gotten a new husband! She did not recognize him. My husband told me he is happier too because he can see his jawline again!

Now, when I am afraid to speak up, I ask myself why am I afraid, what is the worst thing that can happen, as well as what is the best. I can decide if it is a situation where it is worth speaking up and if I can do so respectfully. Some people believe silence is golden; I believe that when we "sweep things under the rug" debris accumulates until we can no longer walk upon it. I love the quote from Dr. Seuss, "Be who you are and say what you feel, because those who mind don't matter, and those who matter, don't mind." I am speaking up more now to share my story, hoping it will help others. Speaking up respectfully and with empathy can save lives!

Setting Boundaries

I have been around dogs more often this year and have learned a lot about boundaries from them. Not only did I dog-sit for a friend, but we got a puppy of our own. I like a very clean home so when I was dog-sitting, I put up boxes so he would not leave the kitchen and possibly have "accidents." To my amazement, the dog stayed within the boundaries I had set for him.

We also hired a dog trainer for our new puppy. At one of the trainings, she told me that *I* needed to let our dog know when he is done training. Training is done when *I* say it is done, not when the dog tells me. The dog trainer stressed this because the dog would push the limits and try to get away with as much as possible. In other words, I need to set boundaries.

I used to think having boundaries, including saying no, is in-considerate or bossy; I also felt guilty or mean if I enforced them. Now I know that setting boundaries is healthy and necessary. When setting them, I ask myself several questions such as, "What does not feel good?"; "Who is crossing my boundaries?"; "Have I crossed my own boundaries?"; "What boundaries do I want?"; "What do I *not* want?"; "Who do I want to have boundaries with?"; and "How have I contributed to people crossing my boundaries and what can I do instead?" This has been helpful when interacting with myself, my husband, other humans, and four-legged friends!

Having A Strong Relationship With Ourselves

Having a dog has also reminded me to accept myself for who I am and to celebrate my uniqueness and stubbornness. We are all made for different purposes and we were all meant to be different.

For example, my sister's black dog passed away last year. She then had an opportunity to get another dog. She found another black dog and her heart was set on him because of his *alpha* personality and because he liked her when she went to visit him. However, when it was time for the adoption, she was assigned a *white* dog with a *beta* personality. She did not want that dog.

I, on the other hand, had been looking at social media groups about dogs for the past two years and was still a little hesitant to adopt one. Then the perfect opportunity appeared, in the form of the white dog that was not a "fit" for my sister! (My sister also helped me get my dog by saying nice things about me to the breeder!)

My point is that we are all different for a reason and things happen for a reason. Since I'd never had a dog before, a beta dog is perfect because he is more "laid back." Even his coloring is the perfect match for our home, while his brother, who my sister adopted, is the perfect match for hers! This is an example of siblings who, though they come from the same parents, are so different and yet perfect in their own way. It is also a way the Universe helps me live in alignment.

The other lesson is that not everyone likes the same things and not everyone will like me either, which is okay with me now. I have learned to love myself and know that I am already approved by the Universe, so I am not afraid to shine bright even though others may try to dim my light.

As for my husband, though I still get upset when he is, shall we say, "less than perfect," loving myself has helped me give him grace and compassion while preventing me from getting walked all over. I also now know it is not my fault for his choices. Progress! Neither one of us is required to be married to each other and we are each financially independent. We are staying together because we want to. He is very smart, handsome, and funny and I just want him to live his best life. I also need to remember he has his angels near him and he has made progress as well.

To help remind me to love myself and to value progress over perfection, I have a "BLT" with "D'BACON":

- The BLT means to Believe, Love, and Trust myself.
- "D" is for Dog. My dog has brought me a lot of happiness!
- BACON stands for:
  - Breathe and Boundaries
  - Awareness, Action, and an Attitude of Gratitude
  - Courage before Confidence, Choice, and Celebrate wins
  - Ongoing
  - Never give up, Now, and New challenges

I Commit To Being Stubborn, But Will Listen!

As I mentioned in *Women Living on Purpose,* these are my personal guiding principles:

1. "Without your health, you have nothing," per my grandma.
2. "Be useful," as said by my grandpa.
3. "Have fun," per my mom. She knew life can be short.

I also believe the most important relationship is the one with ourselves because that affects health, wealth, usefulness, happiness, and world peace!

Since I sold my office last year, I continue to hone my skills as a transformational speaker, coach, and author so I can help others.

I have also been having more fun, including traveling with my puppy, and focusing a lot on my personal life, including my health and relationship with my family, especially my husband.

I will commit to being stubborn and persistent in my values in order to continue living in alignment. However, I will not take it personally when things do not go the way I want. I will remember it is Universe's way of communicating with me and I will pause to listen to what the Universe is telling me! I will remember to value progress over perfection.

I know I have free will, but I also know that everything is connected and I do not live in a bubble. To me it is important to think win-win, karma, have empathy for others, and to surround myself with like-minded individuals.

Most importantly, I will commit to being myself, being powerful, and being happy! How about you?

ABOUT THE AUTHOR: In over twenty years as a chiropractic physician, Dr. Donna W. Woo helped thousands of patients, including professionals, executives, other doctors, business owners, and their families. She noticed that their stress levels; desire to please people; and not living life intentionally often contributed to their pain. When she too became burned out personally and professionally, she took a "pause" and allowed the Universe to lead her in an exciting, new direction. As "Power and Happiness Coach", her main purpose now is to inspire and help people live with intention and cultivate their relationship with themselves so they can create a life of abundance in health, wealth, usefulness, and joy!

Donna W. Woo, DC, LAT, ATC, CCSP®
Power & Happiness Coach, Author, Speaker
YouTube Channel: Dr. Donna W. Woo
Instagram: @drdonnawoo
drdonnawoocoaching@gmail.com

CHAPTER 3

Believing Is Seeing

Carol Collins

L ife's events are simply life categorized in days, weeks, months, years, and phases of high points and low points. When you think about your life, what are the stories you put together? Do you include both high and low points? How much emphasis do you put on each one? A story wouldn't be a story without both, but how much of each?

There's always a story before the story, be careful how you tell yours. Words matter. Your life becomes what you think, what you look at, what you listen to, what you take in, what you pay attention to, what you are influenced by, and whether you do anything about it. Gloss over the low points and emphasize the high points. For much of my life I focused on the "nots"—not enough friends, not enough money, not enough time, not enough appreciation for who I was, for what I was contributing or accomplishing. I was lagging behind and doing things far too differently than my family to feel like I was on a good path.

At the same time, I had fun. I had laughter. I had joy. But if I were to examine it as a flat road versus incline—I was definitely on an incline, always trying to prove myself and falling short, backing up to recover and dismally failing. Gaining balance is what I was doing and then re-engaging but I looked inconsistent and felt the weight of it.

Relationships always got the better of me; I felt them strongly, and fell into them quickly, head over heels. I couldn't find my bearings, didn't know which end was up. Was I in a relationship or not?

Were we happy or not? Did we love each other or not? Why was I there? Should I stay or go? I was a failure, no matter my decision. Not being good enough went through my mind consistently. The thoughts that I had aggravated and accentuated my life's story. You get what you think about.

How do you think about something different? It's hard until it isn't. Damn near impossible until it isn't. How do you get there? By not staying where you are; by making a decision to do the opposite. When everything in you says stay the course but your life says the course is bad you have to look from a different perspective and find the smooth road. If it's under your feet, stay there, notice it, and love on it. Accentuate the positive. If the road is bumpy, an uphill climb, do something different—and meditate.

Meditation...perhaps an overused term. "Quiet me-time" is more apt. People engage in meditation programs that are too lengthy or physically uncomfortable to do them any significant good. The world does as the world does. What will you do? What is the world getting and what do you want? What is available in the world and how do you get it? Meditation—quiet, silent, short, daily, meditation.

A relationship fallout made me fall on my knees one too many times and finally I did an opposite. I moved. Silently, secretly, completely. I took everything that I owned—which was almost everything in our house—and left the state to start over. I now know why.

In the beginning I embraced newness. I discovered there was fun to be had and people who appreciated me. But I wore a mask the entire time—a smile on the outside, hurting on the inside. Then isolation found me. I found it easier, eventually, to be alone with my thoughts than wear the mask. It was hard to smile and laugh until it wasn't.

Relationship troubles were not new to me. It kept happening, in fact. A pattern of behavior that I noticed and did not like. I thought on it often and what you think about, you get more of. I walked away from the relationship yet carried a burden from it, carried loneliness from it—and a little bit of pride. Pride keeps you going. Baby steps are good, sitting still is not. I was taking baby steps yet sitting still all too often in the beginning. My pattern to cope during stress was researching emotional intelligence. I would read and absorb how to balance my emotions. I read about it and gathered a lot of information. I learned theory. It did not help me much, practically speaking.

I did not know about law of attraction then. I knew emotional intelligence and I was seeking that. It seems almost too simple the things that change your life. For me, it was a Facebook group on how to manifest happy. I was drawn to it. It felt good to read about it, it resonated with me. But I was hurting. I was more of a voyeur of the tips and techniques and other people's stories. I did not contribute much. It became a daily practice to engage in a silent way. I read the stories, never clicking on any links nor engaging one-on-one with anyone. Until one day my hand moved and clicked on a video—and I do mean my hand moved. The law of attraction found me that day. I now know why.

It was Esther Hicks channeling Abraham and I was guided to them deliberately. We are all guided in a way that most people simply do not understand. We have a nonphysical Teacher who comes into life with us, stays with us and leaves with us. It is where intuited thoughts come from—and moving my hand that day, evidently. As soon as I heard Abraham's words through Esther the center of my chest became warm. Just the front. It was a buzzing sensation, undeniable, and it captured my attention. It was soothing, noticeable, and peaceful. So peaceful, in fact, that I listened to another video and another and another.

Soon I found myself turning the videos on upon waking up. I made the intention to be guided to the first one. You know how you sometimes let a book fall open, let your eyes "accidentally" land on a passage and you take it as meaningful? That's how I selected them each morning. I believed I was being guided by my own Guide. I now know that I was. I let the videos play one after another. It became routine to have Abraham playing in the background—all day long.

Abraham introduced me to law of attraction and then meditation. There was something in their words, "You don't have time to not do it," that rang true for me. I now know why. I never missed a day and that changed me. Thirty days in I felt better, calmer. Sixty days in people began commenting that I looked happier. Ninety days in I felt like a completely different person emotionally.

Then something intriguing happened, my face moved during meditation. Not as much as my hand that day, but a small motion. Several days later it happened again, several days more, again only that time it was bigger and more of a swaying. It increased each day thereafter until meditation became quieting the mind with a swirling face! I enjoyed it. I had no influence about meditation to even consider that it was a strange occurrence. I simply liked it. At the end of each fifteen-minute segment my face would stop moving as if on que with my alarm. It felt uncanny, like someone was softly asking me to know he/she was there. Nine months into this daily practice something unique happened. My face stopped swirling on cue as it had done each day and then swung swiftly to the left, to the right and to the left again. Slowly, delicately my face then began moving differently; it felt deliberate. It was softly writing in cursive in the air from left to right, as if on a chalkboard. A beautiful, intelligent conveyance about creation, meditation, my life's purpose, and some personal guidance was woven in that first day. I asked who I was speaking with, and they wrote, "We are Jeshua." Exuberant and overjoyed is the only way to describe it. It was two-way dialogue right from the beginning.

Meditation cleared my mind and my life of clutter. A face spelled question-and-answer session and humanity lesson occurred daily. Within weeks Jeshua asked if they could "borrow my voice" and this is when spontaneous trance channeling occurred. They continued personal teaching on the law of attraction, etheric energy, who my Guide team is, why we all have one, and how meditation leads to connecting with them. They taught me that emotional balance comes by way of a clean etheric body.

Meditation is energy work. That's the real secret and here's why; it's like a classroom for the inner mind. The subconscious part of you is the classroom. If you're talking, thinking, listening to music, mantras, singing bowls, television—the door is closed to the classroom. When you stop all of that conscious activity and sit for just a few minutes with no thought, the door opens and the interior you has a direct conversation with your Guide team and life gets better.

It's a conversation that you do not hear; it's not a conversation exactly. It's an influx of Source frequency that softens and heals the bumpy road of life's experience, heals your nonphysical body. There is help and you can have as much or as little of it as you want. Quiet mind, no thought mediation, and your energy body gets cleaned up.

We all have a physical body and a nonphysical (etheric) body, and the nonphysical body is dirty. It's filled with unhappy thoughts and memories. The thoughts don't go away in meditation, but the emotional content softens. It's how your emotional set point changes. It's how law of attraction alters. It's also how patterns of behavior shift, how physical manifestation of stress is healed, how relationships are fixed, how mental blocks are dissolved, how bank accounts grow, and how good ideas and creativity flourish. It's like a dirty windshield, this nonphysical, law of attraction you. No thought me-time allows your Guide team to clean you up.

How do I know these things? It is what Jeshua teaches through me now. That most interesting day when face spelling showed up in my life's experience turned into, in quick succession, trance channeling for them. Through me, they teach what they call The Essential Material: Who they are, where your loved ones go after they pass, and why we're having a physical life experience; The law of attraction and verbal therapy, and how the power of positivity can change your life; The art of directing Source frequency (Chi) throughout your body and how to partner with your Guide team to clean the nonphysical part of you from limitations that life has done to you; and, connecting with your Guide team, improving intuition, increasing clairvoyance—Jeshua calls it ocularity of the mind—and progressing to channeled abilities. They teach about life as you know it and how to change it by combining law of attraction with energy work so you can manifest a life you are wanting—on purpose.

If I could say one thing to Esther Hicks in appreciation for Abraham leading me to mediation and thereby Jeshua and trance channeling, it would be that the clogged pipes are real. As Jeshua teaches it, there is a mesh overlay on our bodies that we cannot see and those grid lines contain a frequency of healing along with the vibration of life. The vibration of discord IS the clog in the pipes, IS our own personal law of attraction. Positivity plus meditation and energy work cleans it up!

Thoughts create things. What you think about you get—and, you get to have help. Meditation and energy work gets you there. It comes about naturally, easily when you combine them both. It's the yellow brick road that we've all been searching for. In those silent moments your Guide team is at work. The more you believe it, the more you think about it, the more your positive law of attraction strengthens. They clean your grid for you, but you have to give them time to do it—that's quiet meditation. Life gets easier, the past gets undone, and the road ahead smooths out.

Chapter 3
Believing Is Seeing

What I now know is "You get what you think about"—only now I end it with a smile instead of a frown. Wherever you are in life there are bumps and there is smooth. Focus on the smooth when you are staring at the bumps. It will serve you every time. Daily, no-thought me-time makes it easier to not look at the bumpy road and then removes it. Healing is taking place; you change from the inside out.

How do you do the opposite when life puts you on your knees? Meditation gets you there. In the silence your Guide retrains your inner mind to think healthy. Believing is seeing. Stick with it. Life gets better when you do, permanently.

ABOUT THE AUTHOR: Carol Collins is a gifted channel, the voice for The Jeshua Collective and is The Pittsburgh Medium. Her abilities spontaneously manifested in March 2019 after nine months of quiet meditation. Through her, Jeshua teaches about collective consciousness, manifesting with ease, health and wellness through natural healing, and intuitive studies bringing out the natural abilities to connect with Guides and Loved Ones in everyone. In 2021 Jeshua channeled 11 books with more on the way. She frequently offers readings, classes, and workshops with Jeshua. She has been interviewed by celebrity personalities, featured in over 20 magazines, and named Top 10 Women to Watch by LA Weekly.

Carol Collins
Original Channel for The Jeshua Collective
thepittsburghmedium.com
YouTube: The Pittsburgh Medium
240-561-1338

CHAPTER 4

My Gift of Healing

Stephanie Kraft

It was the year 2000, and my friend, who I will call Samantha, had just told me of a recent session with her psychic. In the politest way possible, I said to Samantha, "But you are an intelligent woman. Why would you waste your money on something like that, something that's totally fake?" At that time, I didn't believe psychics were real. I didn't believe in *anything* unseen. Her reply to me was, "No, Stephanie, you have to listen to my session. He records them. Just listen to it."

Samantha lent me her cassette tape (we still used those back then) and I listened to the psychic tell her things there was no way he could have known. I was pretty blown away, so I set aside my skepticism and made an appointment. That year had been a rough one for me and it wasn't over yet. I had been having multiple heath crises, some extremely severe, and my life was shifting on all levels. I had quit my job to take an intensive summer course as a pre-requisite for a second Master's of Science degree in Acupuncture. I had moved into a studio apartment in Denver, Colorado to cut costs while not working for those few months. There was a lot of change and upheaval happening.

When I arrived for my appointment, I was completely up front with the psychic, saying I didn't really believe in these things and that I wouldn't give him much information, because I was sort of testing him. Gracious and understanding, he didn't ask me any questions and went right into the reading. What happened next would change my life. He read my heart and soul. He knew things about me that no one could know. He told me that I was a healer and a teacher.

He woke me from a deep slumber I didn't even know I was in.

That night I was in such an ecstatic state that I didn't sleep a wink. *If he could know these things,* I thought, *then there is so much more out there that I don't know about, so much more that is true!* Indeed, as a result of the reading, I was suddenly aware of a vastness I had never contemplated before. As I lay there in bed in astonished awe all night, I was seeing the Universe. I mean this quite literally. My eyes were closed and I was trying to sleep, but instead of darkness it was the Universe that I saw with my inner vision.

Let's rewind to January 2000. I was working in sales at a health club. Four years earlier I had gotten my Master of Science in Health Promotion Management, and while I was helping people get healthy by signing them up for gym memberships, this was not what I went to graduate school for. I really wanted to help people on a very deep level, and not knowing how I was supposed to do that had been a source of inner turmoil. When the psychic told me that I was a healer and teacher, it rang a bell of deep resonance and confirmed something within me that I had never accessed consciously.

I now know my illness was caused by not having found my true calling, and from working in jobs not in alignment with that calling. I was suffering from exhaustion so severe that I was unable to get out of bed in the mornings. Each day, I was late to work; each night I would come home, eat something, and fall asleep on the couch by six p.m., only to wake up at ten wanting to get into my bed for the rest of the night. The problem was, getting up from the couch felt like the hardest thing in the world. Something was very wrong.

My health continued to decline over the months. Desperate, I had started going to an acupuncturist and taking Chinese herbs, but things only got worse. I became overwhelmed and obsessed with figuring out what was going on with me. In the midst of this stressful time, I accepted a new job that made my heart soar and felt in alignment with who I was.

When I attempted to resign from the health club, my boss offered me a promotion to Director of Sales, which meant more money and benefits. I knew I wanted to take the new job, but it was part-time and had no benefits. I had a decision to make. I called my mother and told her about both jobs. My mother, with her own worry and fear, pointed out the downsides and suggested I take the promotion at the health club.

I told her I could make it work. I would get another part-time job to make up for the lost income and it would not be a problem. I knew it, and yet against my own knowing, I took her advice and called the new job to rescind my acceptance. They were very disappointed.

In my new role as Director of Sales, my heath continued to get worse. I was not happier with my life or my work. My soul was not yearning for a paycheck and benefits, it was yearning to help people on deep and profound levels. When we follow the calling of our soul, things fall into place. When we don't, more chaos and dis-ease ensue.

The lesson was that I needed to learn to trust my own inner knowing and not listen to others, especially not my mother. I had allowed her fears and worries to direct my actions, and thus had continued to go down the wrong path. My body would let me know this by getting sicker and sicker.

In July, the month after I saw the psychic, my father was diagnosed with terminal cancer and told he had just a few months to live. Devastated, I finished my summer intensive course then moved from Colorado back to my parents' house in Washington, D.C. I dropped everything, including all concerns for my own ill health, and just focused on caring for him every day from morning until night.

A couple of months prior to his diagnosis, something extraordinary had occurred: I had a spiritual experience while sleeping. This was not a dream, but an actual interaction in the Spirit realm. During this experience, I met with my father's soul. He had been a workaholic and emotionally unavailable, so I'd often felt like I didn't have much of a father. When my soul was face-to-face with his, I released all of my rage at him, a rage that was not humanly possible. I told him that his lack of affection, love, and attention had damaged and hurt me severely. The look on his face and in his eyes was that of total innocence. He'd had no idea that his distant behavior had that effect on me, and he was terribly sorry. I could see his benevolence and purity and knew he had truly meant no harm. I saw all of this, and all was forgiven. In fact, there was nothing to forgive. All we had between us was unconditional love.

I didn't tell anyone about the experience; I didn't even have the words to explain it as I was just awakening myself. Yet this unconditional love translated into our real lives here on Earth. There was nothing to discuss. It was just there, along with the absolute forgiveness. I cherished that time with my father; we bonded and it was precious. The amazing thing is that no one had any idea that he was sick when I had this spiritual experience, yet the healing it provided allowed me to care for him and be with him until the end in this loving and connected way without any emotional issues. I knew it had been divinely orchestrated at the soul level.

There is enough storytelling about the time I cared for my father to fill two books. Suffice it to say that it was a traumatic time on all levels of my being. It was bittersweet for him as well, as he was dying and simultaneously having a spiritual awakening. Walking him through this gave me even more evidence of the value of living in alignment and the devastation that can occur when one is not.

After my father died in December 2000, I collapsed into bed and stayed there for six months. I found a medical doctor that practiced natural medicine and was diagnosed with severe adrenal fatigue. I was twenty-nine years old and fighting for my life. I followed the doctor's protocol, part of which was to rest and have no stress. The resting part was easy, but the no stress part was nearly impossible because I was experiencing severe abuse from my mother, who I was living with while trying to recover. She had been severely abusive towards my father while he was dying and had shifted this behavior to me after he was gone. It would take many years to heal fully from the PTSD that resulted, but in 2001, while still on my healing journey, I went for my first Reiki training and the following year became a certified Reiki Master Teacher. I was my first client, as I practiced energy healing on myself and discovered that I really was a gifted healer!

In early 2001, I had another session with that same psychic over the phone. Remember that I had not believed in anything unseen before seeing him the summer before. Since then, however, I had continued to have profound awakening experiences. Now, while we were on the phone, he said, "Your angel has a message for you." I didn't believe in angels yet, but I listened as he told me my angel was saying not to get any more degrees, that what I ended up doing would be coming from within, like I was remembering it (from my soul). This message was astonishing, especially since I hadn't mentioned that I was planning on entering a Master of Science in Acupuncture program!

It turned out that I was too sick and still needed to recover from abuse, trauma, and illness, so I wasn't able to enter the acupuncture program at that time, but hearing that message from my angel helped me easily release the idea. Somehow I knew I would be a healer anyway.

In the years to come, I would find my healing gift, and all of my "clairs"—clairsentience, clairaudience, clairvoyance, and claircognizance—would open. I would become a hypnotherapist, study several healing modalities, teach Reiki for fourteen years, and go on to help thousands of people in the deep and profound ways my soul yearned for. And because I had stepped onto my path, my body could heal completely; in fact, I never get sick anymore.

Just as the angel predicted, the gift of healing came from inside. For years, I felt a new vibrational energy frequency entering my body. I could feel it vibrating and pulsing through my body every morning as I was waking up. I could feel it swirling through me during the day when I sat still. Then, one night in 2009 during my sleep, I had a spiritual experience on the inner planes. Beings of light were teaching me about healing the human body. I had been gifted with a new healing technology and was being instructed in it. When I woke up, I knew I had this healing gift. I tested it out by doing Reiki, then "turning off" Reiki and just using my own healing gift. What I noticed amazed me! Just doing the healing myself (without turning anything on, like Reiki does), the healing energy coming out of me felt a thousand times stronger than Reiki. I never did Reiki again. My healing gift has been tested as being higher than unconditional love on the David Hawkins scale of consciousness calibrations. I had no idea anything could be higher than unconditional love. I am consistently amazed by this gift of healing and what it does for my clients, and they are amazed as well. This is the gift of being in alignment.

ABOUT THE AUTHOR: Stephanie Kraft, MS, Intuitive Energy Healer and Master Hypnotherapist, has a unique healing gift she received through a series of energetic downloads. Her healing gift calibrates higher than unconditional love on the scale of consciousness. An intuitive and empathic healer, she uses her spiritual gifts to guide her clients into freedom and peace by helping them release issues and return to their true selves. Stephanie communicates with her clients' higher selves to bring through messages and guidance. Her hypnotherapy and energy healing sessions are transformational and life-changing, even in just one session.

Stephanie Kraft
Intuitive Energy Healing and Hypnotherapy with Stephanie Kraft
stephaniekraft.com
stephaniekraft444@gmail.com
202-250-1051

CHAPTER 5

Discipline
The Ultimate Act of Self-Love
Laura Morrice

L ove, that's what it all comes down to in the end. We all want to feel, be, give, and receive it. It's the energy of creation, allowing it to be an infinite source of expansion. I believe we exist to continue the co-creation of the Universe, each of us contributing to the bigger picture by finding our alignment with love, with our God force energy within. Our energy has its own unique blueprint, and it's our responsibility to express this from a place of unconditional love.

Whenever we feel discord in life, that's our higher self signaling that we're out of Source alignment. That churning ache that forms deep in our gut, or the rapid heartbeat mixed with sweaty palms when a wave of anxiety washes over us, are all ways our subtle feelings try to communicate with us.

I spent too much time ignoring my higher self, going against my internal grain of truth. So the hole kept getting bigger and deeper, and I, like most people, fell under the false illusion that I felt trapped with no way to get out, and my ego was only too willing to have me believe this lie fuelled by fear!

Growing up with an alcoholic mother saw me search in all the wrong places to feel more connected. I knew my actions were not leading me anywhere I wanted to be, but I was young and lost. I spent two years severely addicted to heroin, then, through sheer determination and the support of the Universe, I got clean and began to get my life back on track. I healed so much, yet the fear in my subconscious mind lay dormant.

A few years later, still searching outside of myself for love, I once again followed my ego's false promises. It found its way back through that unhealed fear, and for six years I was back in a hole of my own creation, scared and unable to muster the courage and strength to step out of the darkness and back into the light. I was such a shadow of my former self, with no excitement, no creative expression, nothing to get my juices flowing. Within seconds of waking each morning the heaviness of my present reality would flood my senses triggering the tears and emptiness. It was a far cry from the girl who had always had a zest for life and a deep sense of purpose!

Considering I had overcome the heroin addiction through sheer willpower, I felt I'd let myself down by allowing such a lack of control to now be a dominating factor. The turning point came when my best friend introduced me to *The Secret*. It was the moment I took responsibility for everything in my life, the good but most importantly, the bad. I remember thinking that if I had created this world of shit by default, I had what it took to manifest my life of purpose, on purpose, and if all I got out of it were to feel more positivity, I'd have won! The only thing I knew for sure was that I wanted and needed to feel joy and happiness, to fall in love with myself and life again. Anything that didn't fit in with this needed to go or change. The Universe was signaling that it was time to align and shine!

Mindset

Realizing that I was not in control of most of my thoughts was huge. Like most people, I'd believed I was. Now, my higher self was offering a new perspective on what was happening within my subconscious mind. Slowly, the script of my life's conditioning became so brightly lit that I could no longer ignore it. The majority of my beliefs weren't mine, but fragments of other people's opinions and habits handed down through the generations, picked up from a society that was nothing more than broken pieces of half-truths, stuck together with fear, unworthiness, and a lack of self-love. It would be easy to play the blame game with this, but that would not be a productive way of using my newfound awareness. Instead, it would lower my energetic point of attraction, the opposite of what I knew had to happen.

During my journey to find alignment, I've realized that it really is as simple as following the good feelings—a concept sometimes hard to comprehend. Anything worth having in life can't be that easy, surely? It brings to mind phrases like, "No pain, no gain!" which are precisely what the ego seeks to create internal contrast and resistance. And don't get me started on having to justify being worthy or deserving without sacrifice! Even with this insight, I still find myself locking heads with my ego, and though the triggers became less over time, I know I will always be a work in progress. After all, the negative systems I operated on took a lifetime to install. And to complicate matters, mindset isn't just about thinking but a combination of thoughts, matching emotions, and particular actions. So, by choosing to live in alignment with my higher self, the part of me that remembers my God connection, I had to cut myself some slack or face more contrast of my own creation, and to be quite honest, I was sick and tired of that old song. For this change to be successful, I needed to be consistent with the daily mindset work; find the tools that resonated with my energy and would help me align through ease and flow, not pushing harder and hustling. Here I share my top three energy alignment tools for living an empowered life of purpose.

Meditation

Meditation has been the single most crucial discipline added to my daily routine. I had played around with it previously after discovering it during a yoga class, but I never fully appreciated the benefits of daily practice. Again, I had always looked outside myself for answers and, from a young age, had been conditioned (through organised religion) to believe I was separate from God and thus unaware of my internal power source. Meditation reminded me that all the answers we seek are in moments of quiet solitude and contemplation. I like to think of us all as different facets of God force energy, yet we come from the same source, like a perfectly cut, multifaceted jewel. We are all one, and just like a fingerprint or the rings of a tree trunk, it is our responsibility to find and express our sense of self in life.

In the beginning, my daily practice gave me clarity, a more remarkable ability to focus on tasks at hand and a deep sense of relaxation in mind, body, and spirit. It gave me the confidence to grow from the wrong decisions instead of holding myself in the energy of victimhood. It freed me from the shame and guilt that my ego had held me captive with and opened me up to the unlimited potential of what life could be if I could let go enough and surrender to trusting the flow. The more I committed to my practice, the more I became aware of and understood myself and my place in the Universe. Even the wrong turns I thought I'd made became signposts for my journey through life. I had an unsatiable thirst for harnessing my internal power through energy alignment. All of this was reward enough, so when I started to experience astral projection and lucid dreaming as a direct result of my persistent efforts, it further fueled my motivation for discipline in personal development.

As with all new things, it doesn't take much for the new habits to give way to the old, especially when life throws you a curve ball. But as old emotions and paradigms claw their way back in, the joy of alignment falls just as quick and serves as a sobering reminder to climb back on the path of positivity. I have found through my own experience that over time, the number of setbacks gets fewer, and I spend more time on the wagon of alignment than I do off of it. And this can be tied back to following the good feelings. When living in alignment, I naturally follow the ebb and flow of life, rather than trying to control it and getting frustrated when it goes in an unexpected direction.

Affirmations

Affirmations, when done right, can be one of the most effective tools for reprogramming your subconscious mind. I fell in love with them as soon as I began to practice them. Over the years, I have accumulated hundreds of blank writing journals, each page jam-packed with affirmations. Each line written in unison, the words forming a natural order of aesthetic beauty as the ink flows from the pen onto the page, adding to the emotional connection I feel. It is far more powerful to write them out by hand than typing. Writing creates a more robust neurological pathway, meaning better results. Some of my books have the same affirmation all the way through, and I even have multiple journals of the same affirmation; that's for the massive manifestations!

They're not just for writing out, though; never underestimate the power of the spoken word. I love using spoken affirmations when I'm in the car. No one else can hear me, and others can only see me for a split second. I can whip myself up into a frenzy of positivity and scream my chosen affirmation at the top of my lungs, adding to my now point of attraction.

The most important thing to remember when it comes to affirmations is to feel emotionally connected to the statement. The affirmation should create a matching emotion; else, it won't do any good. It will only stir inner resistance and contrast towards the intended manifestation. For example, let us say someone wants to feel more happiness, so they begin to use the affirmation "I am happy." Unless they can generate feelings of happiness as they repeat the statement, no amount of repetitions will assist them in aligning with happiness. It will only lower their point of attraction, keeping them in the same state they're trying to move on from. This highlights the importance of feelings again when it comes to living in alignment.

I have found recording your spoken affirmation and then listening back to it on a loop to be very powerful. There's something about hearing it in your own voice that helps the conscious mind believe it more, reducing any inner resistance and lessening any contrast that may result.

Being in the Present Moment

The past is already gone. The future has not yet happened. All there ever is, is the present moment, and it is in the present moment that we can actualize the infinite power and potential of our being.

It's, without a doubt, a tricky discipline to master because life doesn't condition us to live in the moment. We feel guilty for past mistakes, and as our mind relives these memories, we reactivate the emotional vibration we experienced, bringing the past back to life. Then there is the worry about future events that have not yet come to pass. How much time and energy do we all waste in these one-sided visual commentaries that the ego projects to keep us in a state of fear? For many years my spiritual growth felt like it was one step forward and three steps back because I focused on the things I couldn't change or the scenarios that would never happen. The consequence was a very confused point of attraction in my energy field, which meant the signals I sent out to the Universe lacked continuity. The results in my reality mirrored the internal chaos, which would open a window for my ego to climb back through to begin another attack. How many of you can relate to this yo-yo effect?

The best way I have discovered to counteract this is to find gratitude for the things you have in your now experience. No matter where I am or what happens, there is always something to feel genuine gratitude for. It may be as simple as being thankful for air to breathe, but that is enough to shift the mindset back into a state of positivity, and from there, I keep building on that momentum.

As with all tools and techniques, finding the right way to use them requires trial and error. Our conditioning is never the same as someone else. What works for me may not resonate with you. This is where the individual responsibility comes in to discover and express your unique self. Take inspiration from others as you journey along the path to alignment, but never direction. That is something we must figure out on our own; ultimately, this is a journey of self-discovery and self-love, with the emphasis being on self.

The love and connection, the feelings of wholeness and contentment, all need to come from within us before we can align with them in any other way. And to be successful in the quest for alignment, we need to exercise a certain amount of discipline to achieve it. Self-love is so much more than massages and time-out. It's giving yourself what your soul needs to live in its birthright of sovereignty.

ABOUT THE AUTHOR: Laura Morrice is an energy healer, spiritual life coach, and author. Throughout the years, she has developed and adapted her healing modality to provide clients with unique personalized sessions that combine energy alignment with coaching. One of Laura's gifts is to access the root causes of blocks and negative conditioning that has prevented their true potential and happiness from being realized. She has a passion and calling for teaching others how to harness their internal power by understanding their energy blueprint so they can live a life of empowered purpose. Life without alignment means being a victim of circumstance, and we're all worth so much more.

Laura Morrice ~ Energy Healer and Spiritual Life Coach
facebook.com/lauramorriceenergyhealer
lauramorrice.com
laura@lauramorrice.com
+44 7760 154531

CHAPTER 6

Nos are Power to Yeses

Amy Brock

When the doors closed, I opened.

I was twenty-seven years old and five months pregnant when I begged tearfully for my second chance. I remember being in the dean's office explaining why she should let me complete my master's degree that fall, hoping my protruding belly would sway her. Three years prior, my life had been gutted when I was politely "asked" to take leave from the university. Still extremely ashamed, depressed, and raw to the core, I wanted only to prove myself worthy of what I thought was my calling.

During the last semester in my social work program, I had to write a diagnostic paper on a patient. Since I am a celebrity in a world of professional procrastinators, I (confidently) submitted the assignment after the deadline. Despite my adrenaline-fueled compilation and the "oh shit I better do this or fail" energy, I felt excited to be at the finishing line. I was graduating within days and about to accept a prestigious therapist position at a top hospital in Atlanta, Georgia.

I'd been very savvy (or so I thought) in navigating the messy, student path to success. I had no concerns for my future, as my professors typically let me slide because of my charm and academic merits. I remember the day I wrote the paper, fueled by Pepsi and Snickers bars, my brain pounding from anxiety and yet still assured of its "A" quality as I pressed the email send button.

Upon receiving the paper—again, it was three days fashionably late—my professor asked for the date and time of completion.

Embarrassed by my habits, I made up a story of a glitchy internet connection and asked her to please excuse the tardy arrival. Imagine my shock when she informed me of her ninja investigator skills, then read to me the original date stamp on the word document. YIKES!

I immediately admitted to the "white lie," but despite this—and my profuse apology—she swiftly announced that I would be failing the WHOLE CLASS and FINAL SEMESTER. My warrior spirit bargained for sympathy, gave her a million reasons to pass me, and even got her to admit the paper was of its usual high quality. All I got was a stern no, leaving me perplexed and feeling like the punishment did not fit the crime.

This answer meant no graduation. I would lose the lucrative, elite position that had been handpicked for me and instead work at the bachelor's level, with a much smaller salary. It also meant telling my mentor, who saw me as his protege, that I'd failed. My only recourse was to request a redo (for only three credit hours) after a waiting period of one year.

I was flooded with thoughts and heart palpitations. How would I recover from this? What could I do next? Why would God not want me to complete this plan?

I still managed to land a decent job in my profession, but I did so while angry at everyone, mostly myself—who I now labeled a saboteur and a screw-up. I spent the next three years mastering the art of self-abuse that included—thanks to that great education in psychological pathology—diagnosing myself with a colorful array of mental health challenges. My only comfort was knowing I would one day retake the class and heal that broken college girl.

Then life brought me an unexpected pregnancy.

This crisis forced a decision to go back to my home state of Florida and consider approaching the university for readmission. I still yearned to complete the degree and live out my purpose—which I believed was to become a licensed mental health therapist and open a private practice. The stakes felt even higher now, as a single mother-to-be with responsibilities.

In the meantime, I took a management position at a medical spa in Orlando, which felt logical because I had run this type of business before. A close friend felt led to connect me to the owner, who was also pregnant and desperate. After packing the moving truck alone, I drove the six hours and moved in with strangers. I was worried and had nothing or no one.

Two months later, and after weeks of devoted prayer, I summoned the courage to ask for an appointment with my old dean. I strategized that I could graduate at Christmas and then give birth to my daughter by the new year.

I cried, sang, and pleaded to God as I drove my candy-apple red Toyota up the turnpike to my hometown. Whatever was decided that day, I vowed I would trust and accept the path. After a four-hour journey and fourteen-minute meeting, the answer, shockingly, was still no. The dean had decided with my pregnancy it would be too risky to complete the semester.

Despite my earlier promise to God, I left FSU both dumbfounded and soul broken. I was legitimately an honor student who aced all my clinicals and studies. I was selected to represent the school in an internship where only one percent of clinicians work in the country, and my mentor submitted a recommendation that I was talented beyond my years. Now everything I had worked for was gone. Imagine my gut-wrenching, snot-producing car ride to a foreign home. I listened to every sad song I could find as my therapy and tried to surrender in belief. I delivered my little girl four months later and gave her to a family for adoption—beginning a life-altering process of grief.

To cope with my pain, I became a workaholic and put all my energy into the spa company. What was originally my temporary survival plan became a very successful endeavor. Surprisingly, I made triple the pay I would have as a therapist and became the owner within three years. I never consciously saw the beauty industry as my path, but maybe my soul did. I remember before college saying, "it would be fun to own a spa because my original plan was to go to hair school." The irony is the place I didn't want to be, became the place I had to be.

Over the next decade, I learned the world of entrepreneurship and mastered lessons on persistence, faith, and self-trust. It turned out that my charm, wit, and knowledge of human psychology paid off in the world of sales quite naturally; however, with great success came a big ego, unstoppable ambition, and an incessant drive to win. I had developed an unhealthy, unconscious desire to prove my value through accomplishment, perfectionism, and self-sacrifice.

After my business suffered through what I call "acts of God," I found myself on the floor of my kitchen sobbing. Exhausted, desperately seeking relief, I moved to the couch for a few days, shut out the noise, and again said to the Universe, "Whatever the answer, I surrender in trust to the next path." Also, during this time, I had escaped into a troubling relationship. Needing answers, and on the recommendation of a friend, I decided to call a medium. One of the first things she said was, "You know you are a medium too, right?"

My response: "Sure, probably so," never imagining what that casual agreement was going to ignite next.

Fast forward three months later, and after the same medium visited me from California, I began seeing and communicating with spirit. Three months after that I was studying with a world-renowned medium, still confused by spirit people waking me with touch and enthusiastic conversation. Six months later, I was training with a group of mediums to prove that I truly had this gift and release self-denial. Turns out I was the real deal. Gulp.

Word-of-mouth readings followed, then one day I was approached by a client from New York City to be on a radio show as a medium.

From that moment I became an overnight success, stunned but thrilled by opportunities. Two years later, at the age of thirty-five, I gave up the spa business completely, aligning to what I believe God created me for. Now, I live in New Jersey with a view of the New York skyline and am working as a professional medium and healer, with clients all over the world.

Everything worked out exactly as life was meant to. I got my counseling practice after all—it's just in a different form and perhaps more extraordinary. In addition to my psychic mediumship skills, I am a soul coach, medical intuitive, and business consultant—and each day my art is filled with variety, spontaneity, and the highest forms of spiritual creativity. I am so lucky to witness daily miracles and connect to faith over fear as a lifestyle. I travel and teach my spiritual knowledge to many. I am totally, madly, deeply fulfilled and in love with me, as is.

I have absolutely learned to love my nos as much as my yeses.

Looking to the past, an invisible thread was always pulling me through one door closing, to another one opening. My sociology years provided me with significant knowledge, and I now serve souls without labels and disease models of mental health. My journey of being a medical spa owner prepared me to be unafraid as a spiritual entrepreneur and gave me the training ground for my medical intuition development. Every no and yes counted. Every step created me. Every failure birthed the next moment of what would later be full-hearted freedom—all because I allowed myself to surrender in my deepest moments of hopelessness and hear angels.

I've learned that sometimes when we self-sabotage it's truly our intuition guiding us to honest joy. Trust yourself even when the pain doesn't make sense. Believe that life is trying to help you make your way home, even when you cannot see or feel it. Expect life to surprise you, and know there is no failure, only forward movement to the shift. Our nature will resist the illogical—but do not. Each misstep could be the keystone to the next version of you.

A few years after my first big "no," I was invited to an alumnus gathering for the university. My ego enjoyed thanking the dean for the rejection since I made substantially more than her salary. It is now my belief that she honored a sacred contract that forever healed my life. By trusting herself my soul's destiny was protected. I could not grasp that understanding during the heartbreak. It is so ironic, that I got all the education, experience, and practice essential to be exactly who I would become without having the proof of ever doing so. It's just like being a medium—as there is never evidence validated before I open my mouth to share the message. I just know, go, and live in the twinkling of my life's calling. My life has created itself like a symphony, developing one note at a time, to what is now a masterpiece of music for my soul to sing.

There are no easy ways or magic spells to align to your sincerest form. The secret is that you DO NOT have to figure out that part. You must first decide if you will be created imperfectly, and then recognize when the inspired life arrives. The ideas will drop like rain on a windowsill. The rain will drip to hydrate the soil below, which grows the flowers, that will become you on earth. There is no end or beginning, just connected moments of happenings and endings. We are here to be instilled with the heart power to be changed. We can be refined and designed if we allow the mystery in. The wisdom isn't in the choice, the wisdom comes from the act of choosing. Choose nos willingly, they just might lead you to your purpose in the paradise of Yeses.

Before I sat down to begin writing this, I was yet on another floor crying again to God and saying, "Whatever is next, I'll surrender...you know the rest." I buckled at having to express my feelings and went into full panic mode, much like the night I had to write THE paper. I reexperienced the anxiety, shame, and failure as before, because my life still isn't what I totally planned. Now in midlife, my dreams of having another baby are fading, the desire for marriage is quieting, and my happily ever after isn't. Each time I looked at my life through the eyes of control, God has brought a surprise and that is so hard for a certain psychic (me). I have now decided to let God dream for me.

I know we aren't really choosing outcomes anyway; we are choosing ALL the feelings. Every feeling has an opposite, so if we chose love, we also chose fear. Both experiences are needed for learning, both feelings matter. This is the me who signed up for surprises, plot twists, and amazing spirit encounters. This is me who gave in. This is the person I counted on to carry me to the "real her" and I love that I get to be made.

This is me who is finishing the most recent chapter of my life exploring the world and adoring my villa, overlooking Tuscany. Last week, I was on a Greek island, giving readings to clients by the Aegean Sea. Yeses are great, but nos…they can be spectacular.

ABOUT THE AUTHOR: Amy Brock is a Medium, Teacher, and "The Eye of Heaven," which means, "Omma" in Greek. In seeking a home for her psychic mediumship and counseling roots she founded her professional practice based in psychospirituality. Since 2013, she has been a flame keeper, changemaker, and path finder. She is an enabler practitioner and loves working her magic to build a thriving community for conscious living. As a healing facilitator she builds superhighways to love and is deeply passionate about serving her clients globally. Amy's soul purpose is to modernize relationships with the Divine in ways that work for today.

Amy Brock
The OMMA
theamybrock.com
support@theamybrock.com
917-776-8374

CHAPTER 7

A Phoenix Rising

Brooke Rowe

Are you experiencing your life through filters and untruths adopted from others? Freedom and autonomy come with the process of deconditioning false beliefs and integrating behavior patterns that are more in alignment with your truth. This takes intensive inner work of facing your fears, taking responsibility and accountability for your actions, and lovingly embracing every aspect of yourself. My experiences with trauma, abuse, suicide, and drug addiction were the catalyst for me to begin consciously living in alignment. This required me to heal my deepest core wounds of abandonment, rejection, and shame. The beliefs and behavior patterns associated with the preconceived notions that everyone I love always leaves me, every man cheats, I'm never seen, and money is a scarcity, all had to be cleared and reprogrammed.

Initially, my mental framework regarding relationships was tainted by childhood trauma. My earliest memory is around age four, and the only one of my mother and father together was him chasing her around our house under the midnight sky. He was hitting her, pulling her hair, and screaming that he was leaving us for another woman. I recall my mom drowning in agony in the trailer we moved into, then watching, terrified, as strangers wheeled her away on a hospital bed; she'd had a nervous breakdown. After she was discharged, we moved in with my great-aunt and uncle, who provided support until she recovered. My fondest childhood memories were when my cousins, Jake and Rebecca, were home from college. Both were exceptionally musically gifted and serenaded me with the electric guitar and piano. I adored watching Jake swing about his long auburn hair as he jammed out a favorite Slash solo. Rebecca played melodies on the baby grand as she sang to me. She also taught me cheerleading routines and to stand tall and balanced while flying. They were my role models and I cherish the tremendous love they showed me during that crucial time.

Unfortunately, my childhood trauma doesn't end with my parents. Ages three to five are the most important time in a child's development. It's when they are learning communication skills and cognitive and social development. They start speaking clearly and telling stories in complete sentences. They are most likely to become aware of gender, follow rules, and want to play with and please others. While getting these developmental needs met through play with my cousins, my uncle was getting other needs met through my innocence. As he groomed the lawn, he also groomed me and fondled me on the mower each time he cut the grass. He was so good at molesting me right under my family's nose that he had me sucking his "lollipop" on the couch ten feet down the hall from where my mom and great-aunt were cooking dinner. This continued until I entered pre-school, where I was also molested by a daycare worker. I remember being in the back seat of his dusty yellow Plymouth. He pulled up to an old house, telling me and another child if we told anybody, he would kill us and our parents. Eventually, I verbalized he had penetrated me with pencils. I still can't recall what else he did to us. Charged with numerous allegations of child sexual abuse, he was never convicted since every child was too frightened to testify.

My uncle's conduct was never even reported. He ranked high in the Mormon hierarchy, so it was decided by the women in Mom's family that his behavior would be kept secret. This greatly confused me, as the family knew he had molested other kids—and children from Sunday School visited the home. Thus, my distrust in organized religion was born. The ongoing pain and guilt Mom endured, from Dad's affair to discovering her baby girl was being molested at the same place she felt safe in taking us, plus at daycare, must have been excruciating.

She overcame it and remarried when I was eight, but just a year later tragedy struck again when my grandmother committed suicide by drinking diesel fuel used for Poppy's John Deer tractor. Watching Mom in extreme distress again was crushing. As a result of these experiences, I developed an anxious attachment style in which the associated behavior patterns would later intricately unfold in my relationships. At eighteen, I moved from the foothills of North Carolina to the eastern part of the state to attend college. My father, stepmother, and blended family were also living in the area. Curious about what busy city life and neon signs had to offer, I wasted no time experimenting with underage drinking in nightclubs and rowdy block parties. Yet I quickly got over my culture shock and continued to prioritize academics. My challenge wasn't maintaining average grades; it was maintaining healthy relationships with guys.

Thinking I was being selective with the men I chose to date, I later realized they needed to heal just as much as I did. My first college relationship was thrill-seeking. Searching for an adrenaline rush one summer night, I jumped on the back of a guy's fiery red and yellow motorcycle. He was charismatic, charming, and tall with brown hair and washboard abs; together, we were a modern-day Bonnie and Clyde—both free-spirited and slightly rebellious, we made a hot and steamy couple.

Each month, he rode his crotch rocket the two hundred twenty miles to stay with me at school. We partied together as well as rented mountain cabins and rode horses. Yet my insecurities would flare up when I heard of him talking to other ladies or frequenting nightclubs without me. Soon rumors surfaced of his disloyalty and, immediately, the false belief that every man cheats was confirmed. This quickly threw my life into a turbulent tailspin.

Within a couple of months, my sense of identity dissipated as we tried to mend our relationship. He moved to Wilmington where we rented an apartment together. My insecurities and distrust multiplied daily. Verbal and then physical fights ensued, and I feared leaving the apartment out of shame and embarrassment. Thoughts of not being good enough and abandonment issues worsened. My ability to communicate my thoughts and feelings declined. Without giving Clyde notice, I moved in with my stepsister while he was at work one day. Relieved to be away from the devastating turmoil, my mental and emotional health still spiraled. I completed junior year struggling with cognitive decline. I despised sunlight and I'd sleep for days. The routine of getting ready and going to work in a restaurant a few days a week became morbidly robotic. Suffocating under this black veil of my own mind, panic attacks paralyzed me with fear. Shame kept me from reaching out to anyone for help. When I finally confided in my dad and stepmom, they failed to listen and brushed it off as if nothing was wrong.

Reluctantly, I informed Mom of my mental state. She linked me to a psychiatrist, who diagnosed me with severe clinical depression. The antidepressant he prescribed had the opposite effect and left me planning the details of my suicide. Convinced my loved ones would understand, I went home for our last Christmas together but had to abort the plan when I couldn't find my stepdad's gun. Then I discovered Mom was struggling with issues I'd been unaware of and I knew I had to pull myself together for her. My medication was changed and I regained the ability to feel emotions; the first one being unrestrained fury. Before I knew it they were being numbed again, this time by heavy drinking and Xanax.

Upon learning Mom was in the hospital battling symptoms of bipolar, I was once again consumed by emotions—this time sorrow and guilt. Inebriated, I went to unleash my rage on Clyde and woke up to the musty smell of painted cinderblocks and black bars blocking my path. What in the hell was I going to do with a criminal justice degree and a list of charges, including first-degree burglary? Five days later a dreadful feeling punched my gut: I knew my mom had died, I just felt it. I'll never forget my dad's somber tone when he answered the phone and confirmed my worst nightmare. Mom had shot herself the day before, which was two days before my twenty-second birthday. Indescribable pain violently shattered my soul into fragments. I spent the day of her funeral in the suicide watch cell.

Anxious attachment patterns were exacerbated when compounded with traumatic grief. To live in a world without my mother was unacceptable, so I sold my soul to the devil. I wreaked havoc on everyone and sabotaged all of my relationships. Ending up homeless, jobless, and without a vehicle, I numbed the pain with promiscuous sex, drugs, alcohol, and whatever else I could. My hands shook every morning until a stranger handed me a beer. In one day I upgraded from roaming the hood and staying in crack houses to being chauffeured to oceanfront condos for escort calls. Yearning to feel the unconditional love I was robbed of, I started having pseudo-pregnancy symptoms. Then one night police found me hiding behind a hotel's dumpster after I'd slung all the martini glasses ordered from room service. They committed me to the psychiatric hospital where I sobered up. Shortly after, I found myself in the suicide watch cell again. This time I was transferred to safe keeping in the women's state prison, where I spent three months. Those months saved my life.

For the next eight years, I was in a domestic partnership where I gained some stability, finished college, and started mending relationships. Exploring spirituality and seeking a connection to God, I discovered Reiki. Guided by the spiritual consciousness that animates all living things, Reiki facilitates healing of emotional, mental, and spiritual discord that if left untreated will eventually manifest as physical illness. Reiki also teaches one to master their emotions instead of being controlled by them. Each time after receiving this healing energy I noticed a positive shift in my understanding of life's previous events. Developing healthier perspectives, I was ready to learn to unconditionally love myself and gain control over my life. This would take immense growth.

Since making that commitment, I've progressively been traveling an upward spiral that leads me closer to my truth. This process included getting clean from my seven-year addiction to opiates, followed by alcohol and nicotine. It involved ending unhealthy relationships and creating the space for new ones. Rebuilding a healthy self-esteem, self-worth, confidence, and a sense of purpose took years. Through strengthening my ability to intuit Spirit's messages, I became aware of core beliefs that needed to be restructured. While working with God in this way, every aspect of my life required change including finances, diet, physical activity, beliefs about myself and others, and how I respond to situations. To whom I give of my time and energy also had to be reconsidered. Swallowing my pride at thirty-three, I moved in with my dad and stepmom to completely start over.

To transform beliefs around money I released a scarcity mindset and integrated one of abundance. This required dismantling social conditioning and then collaborating with the true Source of money. Next, as I gradually changed my diet, I was shown how proper nutrition helps heal the body and mind. Then I healed my deepest core wounds of shame, abandonment, and rejection through inner child work and forgiveness. When I acknowledged the belief that everyone who loves me leaves was my ego's way of protecting me, I was able to let go of that damaging attachment. The result of shifting all of these destructive beliefs and behavior patterns was the increased awareness of how to live in alignment. I developed an unwavering ability to know, love, and trust myself. I learned when to surrender instead of grasp for control. My capacity to remain grateful, calm, patient, and to see the Divinity in all things grew exponentially. I discovered a tangible connection to my mom still exists. Most importantly I gained the ability to be in the world but not of it.

Strengthening my relationship with myself simultaneously forti-fied my relationship with God. Maintaining these relationships has brought peace, fulfillment, abundance, and freedom in measures unbeknownst to me. I'm humbled by the opportunities to expand upon my passions in creative ways I couldn't have imagined. Living in alignment has often revealed circumstances or others hindering my growth, and I must choose to limit the interactions or com-pletely let them go. Allowing God's purpose to work through me has facilitated life to provide me with the means, situations, and relationships of every kind to further advance my self-development. Even acquiring the ability to recognize and transform my anxious attachment behavior patterns, plus become secure within myself has been gifted to me through a miraculous sacred relationship. I've learned that attachment to anything is not love at all, but only fear. Attachment keeps trauma stuck in the body, blocking it from being released. To embody my true self, which is the connection to all that is, I understand I have everything I need within me.

ABOUT THE AUTHOR: Brooke is a Reiki Master Teacher, Cer-tified Spiritual Counselor and medium, and has a BA in Criminal Justice. She attended UNCW and Delphi University. Following her mom's suicide, Brooke's determination to break the generational curse led her to further explore the mystical arts and various cultural beliefs. Reiki is the healing modality that helped her overcome her traumatic grief and aftermath. Once able to help others, she worked in the mental health community as a mobile crisis responder in the hopes of saving lives. Brooke now has a holistic health practice in coastal North Carolina.

Brooke Rowe
Healing Begins Within
healing-begins-within.com
timetoheal21@gmail.com
910-279-2214

CHAPTER 8

When Dark Encounters Light

Christie Szpyrka

My vagina was off probation! The rest of me, however, was not. I had spent the last four years believing that I had genital herpes. It all started when I began experiencing sharp abdominal pain and was referred to a very stern OBGYN, who upon review of my medical history suggested I needed to be tested for herpes. According to her, more people had herpes and didn't know, than people who had herpes and did know.

When I went back for my follow up appointment to get my test results, it was revealed that the sharp abdominal pain was a result of bursting cysts on my ovaries that were most likely caused by the birth control I was on. She suggested I switch to a different birth control to "quiet my ovaries." She then coldly delivered the news that I had tested positive for Type 2 genital herpes, while handing me a pamphlet about treatment options. There is no cure for herpes, only medication to prevent outbreaks from happening, as apparently they can be quite painful. I do not believe in unnecessary medication so when I refused the preventative, she quickly left the room with a hard frown on her face, leaving me sitting on the cold hard exam table in complete shock and feeling lost and slutty.

I also decided to stay off of birth control, why would something that caused a problem help it? The cysts never returned, and over the course of the next few years I never had a herpes outbreak. Eventually my mother finally convinced me I should get retested, she was adamant I didn't have herpes. Within a week, I received the test results: NEGATIVE!!!!

I was in disbelief. I called the office, frantic for answers. The nurse I spoke to confirmed that there is no such thing as a false negative, however, there can be false positives. She explained that Mono, which I had come down with the year prior to my first herpes test, is a cousin virus to herpes and can create a false positive. I had never been so happy to have listened to my mother since she was usually the last person whose advice I would heed.

I was elated, bouncing off the walls, texting nearly everyone I knew, "My vagina is off probation!!!!!"

The next day I walked into my rehab counselor's office, "My vagina is off probation!" I had not yet tired of telling people that, but there was an even greater joke to that statement that my counselor was more acutely aware of.

I was in his office for court-ordered rehab. I had been arrested with a menagerie of drugs and paraphernalia and ended up with a felony charge—court-ordered rehab and 120 days of the Albany County Sheriff Work Alternative Program (SWAP) and five years of felony probation.

So while my vagina was now off probation, the rest of me was not.

The past few sessions we had been discussing what I wanted to do with myself. I was 25, delivering pizzas, on probation, and no real idea as to what it was I wanted to do with myself. What I did know was that selling drugs was not the answer.

"You know Christie, you have such an affinity for the idea of natural healing, have you ever thought of massage therapy?" It was easy for me to actually want to listen to what he had to say. My counselor and I listened to the same bands, but he was a professional. He had a career and wasn't getting himself arrested for selling drugs in order to go on tour and follow those bands. The local massage school was having an open house the following week and he suggested I at least go and check it out.

Reluctantly, I went. I had no idea about what massage was or could be. I did know that I was floundering and needed direction.

The Darkest Hour

"I've been arrested 17 times in the past 20 years!" That seemingly proud announcement was ringing in my head as I lay on my cot in the narrow 6x8 jail cell. It was walled in on three sides with bars on the fourth wall so that the corrections officers could see in. I had been in jail for three days at this point, kept in a solitary holding cell, until I could be "classified" and placed in the general population, or "genpop" as the other women surrounding me called it.

We were kept in our cells for 23 hours a day, with one hour a day out to shower and walk around in the yard. We could talk to each other through the bars, our voices traveling down the corridor to each other, bouncing off of the cement walls. With nothing more to do than stare at the ceiling or walls, or read a book that was handed off down the row of cells with outstretched hands through the narrow openings of the bars, there was a lot of gossiping taking place.

The woman directly next to me had been brought in a few hours after I was, ironically, arrested by the same state trooper who had arrested me. She had seen the vast array of drugs laid out as evidence on one of the desks. "I wanted to reach out and eat some of them," She laughed. "Man, I really wish you had!" I said earnestly.

Now it had quieted down, we had all just eaten our dinner, and everyone was tired from full bellies of subpar high school cafeteria-style food and a long day of nothing but yelling conversations to each other. I was reflecting on some of the other women's stories who had been shared that day, but that one in particular stuck out to me.

Her first stint in jail had been for 11 years. Which meant she had been arrested 16 times over the course of nine years!!!!! She explained that she had been arrested for various charges like petty theft and drug possession. She seemed proud of her record, I suppose as a sort of defense mechanism, lest she show any sign of remorse for a life of drugs and discord.

I will never forget how, as I lay there staring at the bare cement wall, the dim light coming in through the dirty windows across the hallway, I realized that if I continued down the path I was currently on, my story would end up in a similar manner. At that moment I knew I had some changes to make.

My mother had done a very good job of protecting me from the world at large, to a fault. I wasn't allowed to "ram the streets" with my friends from school. So once I got my license and a job, I would find every excuse under the sun to get out of the house and explore the unknown world.

For this reason, I loved working. My first job was at 12 years old at my dance studio, helping teach baby ballerinas how to dance on Saturdays. During the summers I worked at the local library. When I turned 16 I got a job at McDonald's and that's when I learned about the real world.

My new friends introduced me to Pink Floyd and The Grateful Dead. Nearly everyone there smoked pot. The manager was on a constant swing of uppers and downers and as a result could be quite volatile to work with. The freedom I was able to have from making my own money was intoxicating. The people I got to meet made life so much more interesting than it was scary as my mother had tried to instill into me.

I was accepted into college and within a month of starting classes I found a job at a local pizzeria. I started out as a counter girl, moving on to make pizzas and eventually I saved enough money to buy my own car, allowing me to deliver pizzas and make a lot more money. I ended up dropping out of college after freshman year as I didn't see the point in paying for a degree I might not ever use, since at the time I had no idea what I wanted to do with my life.

My coworkers listened to a number of bands that I had never heard of before, and traveled all over to see these bands play. I found this lifestyle to be very appealing. The problem was, this lifestyle was expensive, and I was not one to depend on someone else to make my way through life. I had seen how my mother had spent her life trying to find her "dream man" to take care of her, and just ended up living a life of disappointment and sorrow. I was not going to let that happen to me.

I had been selling marijuana for a number of years and it helped offset a lot of my expenses, but it wasn't enough to fund the lifestyle I was seeking. So, having the entrepreneurial spirit, I found a connection for a lot of ecstasy for very cheap. It was a crowd favorite at a lot of the concerts I went to, so my plan was to make a bulk purchase and hit the road, using the funds I made from my on-the-road shop to pay for gas, food, and concert tickets.

I had sold about half of my initial purchase and was headed to Boston for the next show. I had a headlight missing, and when I got pulled over, it was discovered that my license was suspended from not taking care of a ticket for running a red light while delivering pizzas. As a result, my car had to be towed, and protocol stated my car needed to be searched before it was towed. Incidentally, the state trooper found my stash and I was placed under arrest.

The Dawn of a New Era

In Hindu mythology, Ganesha is known as the Lord of Obstacles, most popularly thought of as a remover of obstacles. Lesser known, he also places obstacles in the way of those who are on the wrong path so that they may instead find their correct path. The first time I read that, it became very clear to me that my getting arrested was Ganesha stepping in to set me on the correct path. Subsequently, I crossed paths with my own "tour guide" in my rehab counselor who helped point me down the right path.

So there I was—on probation, in rehab, and feeling lost and unsure of what I wanted to do with my life. I didn't want to go back to college, but I needed to figure out something to do other than work at a pizzeria for the rest of my life and it had been made very clear to me that life as a drug dealer was no longer an option. And so, I went to the open house at the massage school thoroughly skeptical, and I walked out having signed up for massage school with a renewed sense of purpose.

When I think back to all the twists and turns along the way, it is obvious how each decision and resulting life experience all added up to bring me to where I am meant to be in this lifetime. Even learning how to make pizza played a part, as I credit the ability to spin an even crust to my ability to feel imbalances in muscle tissue. Refusing unnecessary medication allowed me to learn that I had been misdiagnosed with a life-changing disease. Getting off of birth control taught me that the body can heal itself when given the time and space. The people that I encountered have steered me down various paths, for better or for worse, that have all led me to where I am now.

As I have journeyed down my own path of healing and self-realization, I have found my purpose in becoming a "tour guide of inner healing" for others who are out of flow and looking for direction and self-healing, hoping to realign with their life purpose. My determination comes from the desire to help other people heal in a way that my mother never could. She had spent her life always longing to find her purpose, which she had associated with finding the love of her life and having babies while she maintained their home and he would provide love and safety. Instead, she was delivered heartbreak after heartbreak, living a life of sorrow, which ultimately ended with her trapped in her own body by a neurological disease. When I think back to my mother's disease and how it progressed, I know that if she had had a more holistic approach to her treatment, the progression of her disease could have been slowed down, if not reversed. I firmly believe that repressed emotion can and will manifest as physical disease.

My mother taught me to be stronger than she was and it is now my life's mission to teach others to find their inner strength and tap into their innate abilities to heal themselves.

ABOUT THE AUTHOR: Christie Szpyrka, LMT is a Holistic Health Practitioner whose path has evolved off of the massage table and into the world of coaching. Her diversified training allows her to provide a safe space for her clients to experience self-awareness in order to promote harmony and self-healing within the body. She is a firm believer that we can heal the world once we begin with ourselves. Her long-term goal is to open a healing center and school that targets modern western medical practitioners and teach them holistic therapies to marry modern medicine with holistic and ancient knowledge.

Christie Szpyrka
Reaching Better Alternatives
reachingbetteralternatives.com
reachingbetteralternatives@gmail.com
315-717-6885

One Thought at a Time
Living in Alignment
with Purpose and Values, Self and Others
Sharon Montes, MD

"I am a neuron in the cosmic brain."
~ student of Dr. Liana Mattulich.

Alignment – Mind, Body, and Spirit

When you read the word alignment, what comes to mind? What do you see? What do you feel within your own body? How and where does alignment show up in your life? For me, alignment initially is vertical. I see it as my role as a bridge between heaven and earth. I also experience alignment on the horizontal plane, my connection with the world around me. As a bridge between heaven and earth, I am connected and in relationship with people, plants, air, water, and land. I open my arms wide and connect to life. In addition, to this heaven, earth, and community connection, there is also a return to center.

This center is in the middle of my chest, under my sternum, the home of my thymus. It helps me balance the boundaries between "me" and "we." As I move my hands up and down to align myself with heaven and earth and open arms wide to connect with community, I return both hands to my center. As I navigate life on earth, this integration of up down, side to side, and returning to my heart center gets me in the here and now and supports me in embracing all as one.

In this chapter we will explore how a commitment to alignment shows up in accepting the material energy frequency range; choosing to live in alignment, purpose, and values and how I align with others who align with oneness using different words. I will share ideas of how we can create greater alignment within ourselves and with others.

Alignment – Material and Energy

In the past I experienced tension when looking at what appeared to be the polarity between material and energy, the limits of being a human and the unlimited capacity of spirit. Looking at this from a different point, I realized that these states are actually gradations of frequency, not polarities.

When I was eleven, while walking a country road surrounded by the dense beauty of a northern Michigan forest, I experienced something called "cosmic consciousness." Beyond words, I had a sense of being light, in light, of light, connected with all life around me.

For many years I contrasted this experience with the emotions and sensations of experiences in my physical body. Because of a yearning to consistently live in this state of oneness and light, I judged my everyday life as challenging and undesirable. This thought was reaffirmed while participating in an abusive marriage and spending thousands of hours caring for others suffering with mental and physical pain.

As a teenager, I read many books on the alignment and overlap between spirituality and science. With time and studying physics, I could intellectually reconcile the perceived opposites. In the same way that light and sound are just varying frequencies, so are physical and energy bodies. I started practicing meditation and Qi Gong to integrate and harmonize those energies within myself.

A few years ago, healer friend Reverend Angie La Rue gifted me with these words: "You know we are souls expressing ourselves in mammal bodies. We create learning opportunities so our souls will grow and evolve. Our mammal body doesn't want to change when we are comfortable." Angie gave me another way of looking at my conflicting experiences. As a physician, I have a lot of wisdom in supporting the healing of our mammal body. As a human committed to growth and alignment with spirit, I was able to accept and unify the tension that exists between my mammal body, with its desire for comfort and tendency to resist change, and my soul that is constantly seeking to grow, evolve, learn, and expand beyond what is consciously known and comfortable.

Spinal Health – A Perfect Fusion of Body and Spirit

In the summer of 1981, while completing some public health work in the jungles of Ecuador, I fell about twenty-five feet and injured my back. While the x-ray led to a diagnosis of smashed vertebrae, it did nothing to alleviate the pain. I couldn't sleep, carry my chemistry book, sit, stand, or walk without significant discomfort. I tried a few over-the-counter pain medicines and herbal remedies, with minimal relief.

The healing solution started with a visit to an osteopathic doctor. Eureka! Within minutes of the manipulation, the pain had decreased by fifty percent. I still remember the joy of feeling better when walking out of the doctor's office than when I walked in and I strive to create that same result in the people I work with.

My long-term healing plan also included a two-year commitment to belly dancing, joyful movement that got me aligned and healthy again.

In 1995 I started my work with Dr. Liana Mattulich. A brilliant human being, she taught me that to optimize my capacity to help others heal I had to have working knowledge not only of western medicine but meridians, chakras, and physics. My work with her involved neurofeedback, wisdom teachings, art, and several mental and physical exercises. One of the exercises was to cultivate a connection with our axis, an energy structure surrounding our spine. As my practices and awareness developed, the qualities of my axis evolved. The colors, sensations, and qualities of warmth, flexibility, and the light changed.

Concurrently with working with Liana, I started to practice and teach medical acupuncture. I learned about channels of Qi, or energy flow in the body. As a western doctor I knew that the fertilized egg forms a ball of cells that gets divided into top/bottom, front/back, and right/left. These divisions are actually some of the primal Qi channels and provide the direction and template for development of our body organs. The first layers that form give rise to our spinal cord, followed by our heart.

Before there is a material expression, there is an energy structure. These residual energy channels, many of which follow along our fascial planes, are still used in the practice of Chinese medicine. In this medicine there is no boundary between mind-body. Emotional imbalance is seen as cell imbalance and cell imbalance is seen as emotional imbalance. Both are healed by correct application of needle, light, sound, or pressure at the correct place along the channel.

LESSONS AND APPLICATIONS

- Alignment is a multi-dimensional, constant process and an inside out job.

- A constant desire for comfort is frequently an obstacle to growth.

- Through mind-body practice and focus on the NOW, my connection and capacity to experience being light is possible, breath by breath and thought by thought.

- I share this heart-centered alignment and connection process with others, by teaching them a standing form of muscle testing that integrates alignment and centering of body energy, they can be guided to make decisions that are more light-filled. Which choice is more yummy? Which choice is more aligned with the highest good? Which choice creates more joy? The body is energized by and will lean forward with that choice.

- Movement is medicine. It requires a commitment to schedule time and repeated practice.
- Structural, mechanical, and emotional problems may quickly be resolved with mechanical solutions. Body pain may be a result of stuck emotions and movement may help release healing. In turn healing emotions frequently resolves emotional issues.

Alignment with Life Purpose – Adventures in Coaching

In 2015 I committed to learning and offering coaching. Although my program originated from sports psychology, I was attracted to it because it has an explicit spiritual orientation and focuses on helping people achieve alignment and connection with their unique life purpose and values. I learned a specific process for defining life purpose, which remains the same throughout our life. The capacity to reduce our life purpose to a specific sentence is very useful and has many applications. For example, my life purpose is to live so that my presence facilitates and celebrates freedom and joy. The coaching system I studied also includes clarifying our values; claiming personal guidelines for living; and identifying the forms of support (emotional, material, etc.) needed for success.

LESSONS AND APPLICATIONS

- Our life purpose is consistent through areas and stages of life. A person's purpose will vary in expression, not orientation. This has been useful in helping people I work with adapt to and navigate life change. For example, mothers dealing with children leaving home learning to express purpose in new forms.
- One useful coaching concept to support healthy change is described by Jonathan Haidt Ph.D. We need to imagine a rider sitting on top of an elephant that is walking down a path. The rider is our intellectual/logical/analytical conscious mind that can see the path ahead. The elephant is the subconscious emotional mind that provides the power

for the journey. The path is our external environment leading to our desired outcome. It has been said that most people have a daily 15-minute budget of willpower. Given the 6-ton power of our emotions, aligning our thoughts words and actions can be difficult. Sometimes the most effective use of our logical mind is to organize the outer environment to make right choice the easy choice.

Alignment of Religion and Spirituality – Unity Beyond Words

In high school, one of my most influential classes was that of comparative religions. We first studied the western religions—Judaism, Christianity, and Islam—followed by eastern religions of Hinduism, Buddhism, and Confucianism. I was struck by the fact that if there is only one God, one unifying force, all the paths that humans have created connect with that God.

Over the last year, I have been drawn to work in a community with a group of powerful people aligned with spirit through Christianity. My use of language has created some tension in these new friendships.

My reluctance to speak of God as father, but in terms such as mother/father, Source or Creator, has created distrust in some of the people I am working with. I have grappled with this, talked with friends and work partners about it, and brought it to light. I have found that there is a spectrum of how my new friends connect with God. One woman I met believed that crystals and the healing a shaman facilitated were the devil's work. There were others who, when they use the word Christ, or God, it is totally in alignment with my experience that the Christ experience expressed.

I have also come to accept that in the same way that these people are being authentic in their connection with God—beyond religion—I too have to be authentic by holding the vision and the prayer that everyone I care for is aligned with Source energy, because that is what I perceive as the Source of the healing. I will continue to be nondenominational in my vocabulary, and I will continue to hold the thought that people do not have to have a personal relationship with Jesus or the Bible in order to know or express that which I call God.

I am at peace with my Christian brothers and sisters and love the learning we are doing together. We are going beyond language in service to create something greater than our individual minds and hands could create alone.

LESSONS AND APPLICATIONS

- Beyond the words is the experience of frequency, unity. My heart is the best source of orienting this way

- How can I create that experience of unity while excepting difference of opinion? I can commit to action and collaboration with my partners without total agreement at the word level

- Beyond my personal relationship with a master or a teacher is my personal responsibility to be a steward of my thoughts. Is my mental chatter serving to create a space that we can all live and grow in? With the goal of feeding my monkey mind a nutritious banana I frequently will align my body-mind using various exercises

  - Tapping my thymus – repeating I love Me! I love We! HA HA HA and HEE HEE HEE

  - Holding thumb to middle finger – repeating "I am the infinite and eternal here and now"

  - Walking – repeating on syllable with each step "I am healthy, wealthy, happy, wise, and strong"

Alignment – Point of View

One day many years ago, while sitting at the breakfast table, calming myself after an argument, I had an epiphany. As I looked down on my teacup, I saw one side with a smooth surface and the other with the handle. At that time, I was married to a man with very different ways of communicating and looking at the world. It occurred to me that our worldviews were as polar opposite as the teacup's smooth and handle sides. We were experiencing the same reality, two very different ideas. Looking down on that cup from the THIRD point of view, I could observe and unify both perspectives.

That became a new way of looking at many areas and events in my life. What point of view takes me out of polarity and helps me create unity in my perspective? What point of view helps in creating alignment with self, Source, others, and the world around me? Who and what am I aligning with and why? Wishing you the joy and freedom of your alignment with all that is dear to you.

ABOUT THE AUTHOR: Dr. Sharon Montes, MD, is an internationally recognized pioneer in the field of integrative health and holistic medicine. In her thirty-seven+ years of clinical experience, she has served as Medical Director for such prestigious health care facilities as The University of Maryland Center for Integrative Medicine; University of Colorado - Rose and AF Williams Family Medicine Centers; and North Texas Area Arlington Community Health Center. Committed to helping community leaders and compassionate warriors stay healthy, Dr. Montes continues to share her expertise as a lecturer, course director, and in radio and TV interviews. Currently, her primary focus is offering Living Well Resilience Programs to help others live with greater health, happiness, and efficiency.

Sharon Montes MD
livingwellwholehealth.com/PQ
support@livingwellwholehealth.com
970-682-4885

CHAPTER 10

Awakening Through Inflammation and Shakti

Rae~Ven S. Barnard

rowing up, I was never told that I had the power within me to physically heal and protect myself. I was told the opposite—not only that the power was outside of me, but I had to be worthy of it. It's no surprise then, that as I look back on my life, to see how disconnected I was from my power, and how blocked my creative energy was.

Because of this, I "powered" through life, relying purely on outside energy sustenance, never really listening to my body, flow of energy, or soul, or even knowing what that meant. I was more concerned about outward connection, being socially accepted, people-pleasing, and laughing at all the jokes.

I would often experience bodily symptoms that I now know was me viscerally experiencing subtle energy. As a kid I was shy with social anxiety which always made me feel socially awkward, I had a very sensitive digestive system, and was diagnosed with spastic colon. Super-empathic, I felt everything but had no understanding of what I was feeling or confidence to explain it. I always felt mis-understood and that I was never taken seriously.

I had a lot of energy, and my expression of it usually came out in bursts of emotion, be it excitement, anger, or orneriness. I learned that extroverting was healthy and that introverting was not healthy, so I denied my natural introversion early on. I was grateful for the vast space of country living. Freedom with Nature was the saving grace for my bigness of energy and feeling.

I expressed my energy through my rebellion, finding it hard to stay inside the boundaries that life gave me. I grew up making the phrase "I can do it by myself" quite popular. I had a strong heart and mind that always needed to go in a unique direction, while at the same time I often felt I only had the ability to follow. This is the inner torment that grew inside of me. I learned to deal with it and keep following, which only made the silent stirring of my power and my instinctive wild soul grow stronger.

As an empath I was aware of acting in a way that created social comfort. My family preferred to joke, tease, and laugh. It was all in love, but through this, I learned to suppress my energy and deep emotions, as there didn't seem to be space for them. Somehow I knew or learned that what I felt so deeply would disturb the comfort of others. I understood deep sensitivity as something to fix with medication. It didn't quite fit in.

My spiritual life during early adulthood was fairly nonexistent, but in 2008 I started to make some real changes in my way of living, with awareness of self-care and sparking curiosity to exploring power within.

My childhood was grounded in spirituality. But it was the spirituality of religion, and my heart was searching for something that religion could not fulfill. My ex-husband and my ex-in-laws really opened me to that something, with depth psychology and phenomenology, esoteric ideas and soul talk, and plant medicine.

That same year, I had a dream that was the seed of my kundalini activating, which would not actually occur until two years later. In the dream, I was walking and laughing with a group of people. As we turned down a hallway, I heard someone crying in the room we were leaving. I left the group and went back toward the person, who was hunched down in a corner hugging their knees. This person was me. I nestled up next to myself and said, "It's all going to be okay, I'm here now, I'm not going anywhere."

I knew it was a medicine dream and had a reverberation into 3D life, that something had seeded into my reality. It had manifesting power. I was no longer following the crowd, and I had heard the cries of my soul.

Around the same time as the dream, I began expressing inflammation through my eyes and was diagnosed with Uveitis. Something deep was stirring in me and I had no idea at the time.

Between 2008 and 2010, life was good for the most part. I worked for an Italian fashion designer and got to wear/promote beautiful wearable art and fabrics and travel. I was successful in my work, I lived a comfortable life in a home that I owned in Chicago, I was married, I was in my youth at thirty-one. I was healthy aside from these Uveitis flare-ups from time to time. They were no light events; it was inflammation that really took me out of my life with the pain and visionary limitations. Not something I could push through very well, as I was used to doing. I would typically wear an eye patch as light caused most of the pain.

This was a time in my life that forced me to face my natural introvert. The darkness soothed the eye and inflammation pain, like a cooling, relaxing support that allowed my energy a chance to calm. My rhythm was changing and my body was beginning to talk to me in very noticeable ways, needing my attention and changes in my routine and in my relationship(s).

Then, in the spring of 2010, an outside event occurred that fully activated that dream seed. It was music and ecstatic Creative Fire energy. It was an electrical ignition through the ethers direct to my soul. Like a strike of lightning, it opened my blocked creative and sexual energy, instantly activating kundalini. For a solid month after this activation, I could not eat or sleep, yet I had so much energy and felt better than I ever had. I was also emotionally, sexually, and creatively opened and charged. I felt different about my life. It suddenly didn't seem like my life any longer.

Shakti, Creative Force Power, was active within me, and it turned life as I knew it on its head. Over the course of two years following my spiritual awakening, my husband and I divorced, I left my career in fashion, and I was instantly in tune to the world of energy. My life was unfolding as a series of magical and synchronistic events, even through all the pain of an entire path ending.

The intense emotional distress that came from my life being turned upside down by this tidal wave of energy triggered me on a genetic level. It awoke lineage suffering in my body; a dormant gene I didn't know I carried. The Uveitis I was previously experiencing became systemic throughout my body. I was diagnosed with Reactive Arthritis. I was out of work for months, unable to move or see very well.

My body was inflamed and literally stopped my life in its tracks. My body's wisdom was becoming my new center. My pace was changing forever. I was forced to go slower and to go inward, listening deep, immersed in the darkness, as well as the darkest night of my soul. My heart had arrived at an edge of everything I knew, or thought I knew. I plummeted into the Unknown abyss of my infinite Being. I had never felt so alone, nor had I ever been so close to my power and deeply felt emotion, and it was in this depth of grief where I felt the Void touch me. That was my first experience of Divine Grace in the depth of despair and realized the truth that I was actually never alone. Then the words came that called me into the act and life walk of surrender: "Letting go of who you think you are to become who you truly are."

Inflammation became my ally and adversary. A call from the Body to come into a new and more intimate relationship with it, cultivating the space and love needed to embody what was awakening in me, slowing me down tremendously, and knowing the pain as a portal for deeper healing.

I began to hear Nature as my guru, guiding me into the practice of Presence and Surrender. The Trees taught me to focus my mind and energy and to remember my Earth-Body. In Chicago, I did not have much Nature to access. I often sat with the trees that lined the densely populated neighborhood streets in the back of my house, in answer to the early morning call to sit with Tree as ritual before going to work. Sitting with my back against the trunk, I focused on breath. The Trees would guide my energy and awareness to a center point of connection/contact, typically around the center of my back. My practice was to focus my energy here and breathe. The Trees were teaching me to retrain my flow of energy, engage breath to alchemize pain and emotion, to create space from within, introducing me to Heart Center as a portal for alchemy, multidimensional healing, and unity consciousness.

At a time when inflammation pain dictated my life, the Trees showed me what to do with it and how to align my bodies of being. Mother Earth showed me how to listen to my intuition as my power. She reconnected me with my boundaries, the Elementals, and to Presence as my spirituality. Grandmothers of the Cosmos showed me the healing power of surrender to Shakti energy.

Over the years I have been in school with myself, arthritic inflammation, and Shakti, teaching me how to allow its flow in my body. My nervous system was unable yet to hold and wield this power, resulting in inflammation throughout my body, yet I knew my body was growing in intelligence with Spirit. These teachings and this journey have taken me into mental, emotional, and sexual healing, ancestral and past life healing, and DNA healing. It has taught me that inflammation is energy that is trying to awaken in the body, and to be embodied. My body has remembered how to embody orgasms and ecstatic energy to support my physical health and overall well-being. The intelligence of my body is remembering the truth that inflammation is energy that can be embodied for self-healing and expansion.

I recall the precise moment this truth was fully remembered in my body. By now (ten years into living and learning with Shakti), I was familiar with detecting inflammation in my body well before any body part inflamed. There was a pattern I had discovered in my "cycles of becoming" with inflammation, starting as a sudden burst of energy in my body, turning into a depression and deep plummet, becoming a weight of exhaustion and grief, then, at the end of the cycle, gathering at the top of my spine. Indeed, I knew this pattern of energy well, and it was headed to inflame my eye as Uveitis. When I woke up the next morning, my neck caught as I lifted my head to sit up. Excruciating pain with each turn. My body had stopped the inflammation in its old tracks. It had changed the path of this pattern, changing the tracks.

For a year straight, I showed up for myself every single day to do neck rolls and breath-work, often through tears of pain, bringing all this awakening energy into embodiment. I was present with the pain and it had become my portal of renewal. I was dedicated through Self-Love. I knew I was on the other side of something. My body had strengthened and remembered to redirect the flow of energy away from my eye. I felt empowered through inflammation. I knew now I had achieved true alignment in my being.

I now live with fully activated Creative Force Power/Kundalini/Shakti. I live with the awareness of what triggers awakening energy in me and have learned and continue to learn how to live within these boundaries. I surrender and allow the Flow. The Flow is a sacred dance of my unique journey with Co-Creation. There are many practices that support my alignment with Creative Force Power, but I believe Self-Love is all one truly needs.

I ultimately see my life as a liberating practice of surrender through Heart Center. Surrender can be so big and vague. Surrender to what, how, and why? I surrender to my body's unique

Wisdom. I surrender to the Truth of the moment. I become present with Grace and I feel what is arising. I develop relationship with Nature, Earth, and Elements through deep listening. I practice Heart Center Presence and the alchemy of Self-Love. I surrender mental, overpowering energy to Heart Center. I surrender my energy to the Flow that is Shakti and the sacred dance with chaos. I am frequently humbled while fully in my power. I have embodied the truth that pain always opens up through surrender, the ego releases resistance, and Shakti can ease-fully flow.

The waking natural wisdom of living in Co-Creation may come in as a subtle awareness or intense force, but it is always a deep stirring of the Soul. It is always the messy, painful, beautiful, healing journey of becoming who you really are over and over again. Living in alignment is a practice and never-ending journey of discovering the power of your presence and capacity to be true to You through all the changes, forever.

ABOUT THE AUTHOR: Rae~Ven is a Soul Midwife, subtle energy therapist, plant spirit medicine practitioner, ceremonialist, and unity consciousness guide, certified in shamanic energy medicine, Ayurveda Yoga, and Reiki. Rae-Ven guides others through the deep heart portals of transition, into the embodiment of new realities and empowerment through understanding their Wholeness in relationship with Nature. Grief Alchemy and Heart Center Presence are at the core of her magic. Twelve years ago, a powerful kundalini-igniting experience landed Rae~Ven on a new life path dedicated to self-study with Shakti, personally transforming her relationship with inflammation and depression, from pain into empathic empowerment and awakening energy.

Rae~Ven S. Barnard
Heartfelt Whole Self, LLC
heartfeltwholeself.com
heartfelt.wholeself@gmail.com

CHAPTER 11

Aligning My Life
with Heart and Soul
for the Greater Good

Bernadette Bloom

In the mid-1980s, I was Assistant Director of a sports medicine facility in New York. While treating the injuries of others, I struggled with my own very painful and unstable back. It was hard for me to brush my teeth, stand straight, make love, or get up comfortably from a chair. I began practicing the exercises I had been teaching to my clients and, in addition, received traction, hot packs, ultrasound and electric stimulation, yet I did not improve.

I had been a practicing physical therapist for over ten years, I was well-read on the current treatment protocols—so why was my back not responding to them? Was I destined to have this horrible pain for the rest of my life? Was I going to need surgery?

I had seen so many people have surgery and continue to experience the same level of back pain. At a continuing education class, my instructor told me I was an accident waiting to happen—that if I did not do something very quickly I was headed for serious knee trouble. *My knees, too,* I thought. *They don't even hurt!* I was embarrassed, afraid, crooked (from the pain) and felt lost. It seemed I was falling apart.

Then a colleague directed me to the College of Osteopathic Medicine at Michigan State. The osteopaths there believe that the body is a self-correcting mechanism, if given the correct input, and that the entire body is a series of interconnected systems. As I learned this approach, and at the same time received treatment, I started to feel better. I began to have hope.

Briefly, the craniosacral rhythm is a rhythm of health that flows through the body from head to toe. When it is interrupted for one reason or another (trauma, stress, grief, fear, anxiety) an imbalance or a dis-ease process begins. I learned that whiplash injuries can cause many types of damage, including neck, back and even gastrointestinal problems. I learned that ankle sprains (I can't tell you how many times I sprained my ankle as a kid) can cause knee and back injuries. But, most importantly, I learned that when a person's body begins to hurt, it is sending a cry for help. Pain is a great masquerader, and if you chase pain it becomes just that—a chase. Many times, while you are busy chasing the pain, you miss the cause of the dis-ease and/or imbalance.

By 1992, I was feeling better and life was good. I was happy—I was making a difference. Then people with more complex imbalances began coming for treatment: people with diagnoses of diabetes, multiple sclerosis, autism, Parkinson's, auto-immune diseases, fibromyalgia, chronic fatigue syndrome, cancers, HIV, attention deficit, reflex sympathetic dystrophy, traumatic brain injuries, and migraines. They felt better when they left my office but their relief did not last. Again, I felt powerless—I wasn't making a lasting difference. What else could I do? Where were the answers?

That same year, I learned about Esoteric Healing from a friend of mine and started to take classes. Esoteric Healing is an energetic modality based on the Tibetan Djwhal Khul as channeled by Alice Bailey. There are twenty-six books written on this subject. Through this work I began to understand the emotional, mental, and spiritual aspects of a person and how these aspects impact their overall physical health. I continued studying but fearing I would be laughed out of the medical profession, I did not share with anyone what I was learning.

I had been studying Esoteric Healing for two years when one of my manual therapy clients asked, "Can't you do anything else to help me?" Her condition had greatly improved, but she was still not where she wanted to be. I told her about Esoteric Healing and asked if she would like to try it. She agreed, and felt better after the first session. Though I was amazed and thrilled by her response, I didn't understand it. That experience pushed me further along in trying to understand the nature and workings of the human constitution. I wanted to know why some people heal and others don't, and how I could help people like myself who had not benefited from more traditional approaches. Again, as I was learning this work I was also feeling better and better. So, I began to apply the Esoteric teachings to those who had been coming to me with more complex imbalances and they began to get better as well. Once more, life was good and I was happy. I was making a difference.

In 1994 I had my first experience with PTSD, after my sister Colette, who had suffered from mental health challenges, used my then-husband's gun to take her life. It was a turbulent and scary time, for sure. I remember driving to the bank and ending up at the post office, not knowing how I got there. Then I started having a really hard time sleeping and when I did manage to fall asleep I was having horrible nightmares. I was shaking during the day, I could not focus, I was bouncing checks. My relationships were falling apart. I felt hopeless. I tried psychotherapy, EMDR, twelve-step programs, homeopathy, Reiki, Therapeutic Touch, shamanic work, healing touch, and Polarity, to name a few, without relief. Then, nine very long months later, I had an advanced Esoteric Healing session and literally felt the PTSD come out of my brain and my body. I felt normal again. I could function again.

My treatment model today is to combine manual therapy with Esoteric Healing/Energy Medicine. I ask my clients to give me three emotional things they have NOT been able to resolve on their own. I evaluate a person's entire being from head to toe, decide what is out of alignment, what is weak and what is tight, on physical, emotional, and mental levels. I begin each session by making an energetic connection, also known as an alignment and attunement, with Source energy which has many names (Universal Life Source, Higher Power, God, Jehovah, etc.), and ask for the highest and best good to happen for the person. Then, using an ancient Tibetan energetic technique, I first balance the energy centers or chakras of the body to get a baseline of where any restrictions are and what is needed. The nervous system of the body is balanced next. If the person's energy is low I balance the places in the body that bring in restorative and extra support, like the spleen. Next, I assess which emotional issue is the most traumatic and where this issue is stuck in their energy system. In most cases, it is stuck in more than one area. I think about the issue and my client thinks about the issue, which makes the energy system contract; then, using healing energy I balance the areas of processing and areas to let go of the trauma. As a result, the person's energy expands, they feel lighter and are able to breathe better, and their body feels less tight. In many cases they will be able to reduce the amounts of medicines they're on. Then, with their help, I allow their body to come back in alignment. People respond in a positive way—they begin to heal as opposed to "being cured," which is an important difference.

One day while in session and totally focused on my patient, I heard, *You can continue to see one person at a time and that would be okay, or you can go back to school and learn how to teach and you will help thousands. What are you going to do? Choose, and choose wisely.*

That didn't sound like much of a choice to me! I could treat a few individuals myself, or I could use these skills to teach many at one time, who could then help themselves and so many others.

In 1999 I completed the training to become a teacher of Esoteric Healing/Energy Medicine and am now one of only ten active teachers in this country.

In 2002 my mom fell, broke her hip, and was told she would never walk again without a cane or a limp. I left my beloved New York and headed to Naples, Florida to help her. While there, I took a job in traditional physical therapy to support myself…and used Esoteric Healing on my mom, leading to her full recovery. Anyone visiting my website can watch the video of Mom dancing around the pool in the highest heels possible!

Fast forward to April 2010 and an epiphany I had while, of all things, rollerblading. I realized I needed to make some serious changes. I called upon the Spiritual Masters (actually, I demanded that they help me) and, *within hours,* my life changed dramatically. By August, I was back in my beloved New York, but I was broke, practically homeless. I got another job, only to be fired within a month for being "too holistic." I started walking the streets of Chappaqua—a hamlet in Westchester County, north of the city, volunteering to treat people for free. The spiritual masters guided me once again, this time to open an office in Chappaqua. By this time, my mantra was (and still is), *"I serve the world, I have fun, and the money is here"* (notice it's all in the present tense). I have come to realize that it was no wonder having a mantra like this, that the spiritual masters put me back in one of the planetary centers of the world (the other ones being London, Geneva, Tokyo, and Darjeeling). These are the main vortexes where the energy comes into the planet.

My journey now is to help empower as many people as I can to participate in the care of their health and well- being. My dream is to teach the principles of Esoteric Healing/Energy Medicine to as many people as possible so that their lives are happy and that they are making a difference for their loved ones, their communities, and the world. And that, for me, is truly living in alignment.

ABOUT THE AUTHOR: Bernadette Bloom is a medical intuitive, teacher, and practitioner of energy medicine based on the writings of D.K. from Tibet. She is president of the non-profit JJ Esoteric Foundation and founder of the Center for Aligned Healing. Bernadette has studied osteopathic principles as well as Tai Chi and Shamanism, and she combines Eastern and Western traditions in her practice, helping clients throughout the world. Her vision is to serve the world and to empower as many people as possible in their life and health. She was part of an NIH study to heal glioblastoma multiforma in 2001 and has developed a healing program for fibromyalgia, PTSD, diabetes, and breast cancer.

Bernadette Bloom
Center for Aligned Healing
theesotericbloom.com
bernadettebloom8@gmail.com
239-289-3744

CHAPTER 12

Trust Yourself &
Your Path Will Be Revealed

Carrie Asuncion

I had done everything I was supposed to do:
- Get good grades. ✓
- Go on to get a college degree. ✓
- Negotiate a good-paying job. ✓
- Get married. ✓
- Create a loving family. ✓

My husband and I worked hard to make everything look perfect—we threw large parties, placed the kids in private school, and took frequent trips to exotic locations around the world. I stayed home to raise the kids, and my husband traveled the world as a sales manager. Yet beneath the surface, it was a very different story.

For years, I had laid in bed, more nights than I care to admit, trying to figure out a clear exit path out of my twenty-seven-year marriage. My sons and I had been walking on eggshells for much of that time as my husband frequently spiraled into depression, becoming more distant and controlling as time went on. The kids and I felt judged and disrespected by a hostile tyrant in our seemingly together home.

My voice was stifled and dismissed. His impulsive whims beat the family drum. Only in fits of outrage could I raise my voice enough to let my true feelings out—"It's *not okay* to put down people, especially our children—we stand for respect." "We should downsize our home, simplify, and *live within our means.*" All these messages fell on deaf ears. We had an image to maintain.

Freedom, growth, and deep connection have always been my top three values, yet I had suppressed them all during this dark period. I felt hopeless, like a pawn in my husband's game of maintaining outward appearances at all costs. I did what was expected as a dutiful wife and mother—acting as tutor, driver, nurse, mental health worker, cook, social coordinator, and housecleaner—yet I didn't feel valued. I was so busy taking care of everyone else's needs and wants that I had little time to consider my own. At one point, I had even contemplated ending my own life.

Every time I thought of leaving, the inner ping-pong match would begin, with questions like, "What will others think?" and "How could I ever stand on my own financially?" It had been eighteen years since I'd been an equal wage-earner as a Human Resources executive.

I worked harder, and lost progressively more sleep, as I pushed my body to extremes. Professionals told me, "STOP carrying the load," yet I persisted. *If I only tried harder, things would work* and everything would be okay. In the process, I lost myself.

My whole life, I had poured my love and energy into making things work, often second-guessing myself in the process. I also fully embraced the American ethic of hard work equals success. Hypervigilance and over-caring had contributed to a number of health issues—asthma, weight gain, adrenal fatigue, thyroid problems, and low energy.

Hadn't my advanced degree in psychology prepared me to make relationships work? There must be a secret code that I hadn't yet deciphered.

At the same time, I felt robbed. Was it too much to ask to have a partner who had my back? A friend who could share life's ups and downs? I yearned for deep connection and intimacy, yet more often than not, I was left clutching at tiny crumbs of affection. As an intuitive, I couldn't understand why I wasn't getting a clear picture and so I uttered a simple prayer: "Show me!"

I can vividly remember the day my prayers were answered...

I was sitting on the porch overlooking our large, meticulously landscaped front yard. As the sun was setting, I savored a moment of peace before I made dinner for my sons. We were always in motion—something else always needed to be done...yet for this moment, I paused.

The next day I was leading a transformational retreat. Later, as I made final preparations, I remembered the stack of mail from the past week and went to open it. I knew I would be judged if I didn't take care of this detail before my husband, who was away on business, returned. As I flipped through the mail, I saw something that caught my attention—a letter from the IRS.

I called my husband to let him know, as it may need his prompt attention. He asked me to open the letter as he stayed on the line. I ripped open the envelope and felt a jolt of fear and confusion as I scanned the tax return, which stated that we had withdrawn a substantial amount from our retirement accounts, meaning a hefty tax bill. My legs began to shake, and I fell into a nearby chair.

He quickly responded that I must have misunderstood, and he would deal with it when he returned, to which I loudly replied, "NO—we will talk about it now!" I recall my younger son peeking through the window, wondering why Mommy was raising her voice. I asked him to tell his brother to start making dinner while Mommy and Daddy chatted.

Over the next few months, piece-by-piece, I discovered that this was not an isolated instance. In fact, for the past four years my husband had been withdrawing funds to cover gambling debts and other questionable expenses. With growing horror, I realized that all we had worked so hard for was being flushed down the toilet. Our seemingly idyllic life was quickly crumbling.

Yet, it was perfect! Thirty days prior, I had prayed to "be shown" and now I had. I was asking myself why I hadn't seen this coming. I was a smart, educated woman who'd held high-level positions and ran a household for years. Then the puzzle pieces fell into place: I remember at age nineteen ending our friendship after he lied to me—a detail I conveniently forgot when we reunited four years later when I moved to Silicon Valley. He was charming, attentive, and knew how to have fun—money was no object. Later, there were numerous evenings out with his friends, playing poker. Like the famous frog in hot water metaphor, I hadn't seen the warning signs until I was so far in that I couldn't easily jump out. I was also reminded of a Maya Angelou quote: "When someone shows you who they are, believe them the first time."

As time went on, and I did my inner work, I saw how I was equally responsible for the betrayal, because I had first betrayed myself. I had not listened to my inner voice but instead shoved it aside each time I did not speak up for what I knew was right. I had not taken the time to get to know my wants and needs, to pause and reflect and access *my* deeper truths so I could express my opinions. Add to this my inner drive to achieve and my need to people-please, and I had the perfect recipe for disaster.

At a loss as to how to move forward, I turned to my spiritual advisor, who asked, "Is *he* (meaning my husband) your source?" "NO!" I replied, "God is my source!" Then, as I tuned in to my inner guidance, I heard—"*You will find a way through this, and you will create a life even better than the one you left behind.*"

Over the next few years, I experienced the various stages of grief: denial, anger, bargaining, depression and, eventually, acceptance. He wasn't going to change, so I had to, if not for my sake, then for my children's. In fact, something inside told me that if I didn't get out now, I would get sick and die. I also couldn't continue in good faith to coach others to create a life they love when mine was falling apart.

Even as I went through the painful process of ending my marriage, I created a road map for myself by asking the same questions I asked others.

- **What do I *really* want?**
  A loving, conscious, simplified life with deep connection and supportive people.
- **How do I want to feel?**
  Energized, abundant, and deeply connected.
- **What will I need to release?**
  Self-doubt, toxic people, drinking too much to numb the pain.
- **What do I need to embrace?**
  Self-care, self-love, slowing things down to heal.
- **What small steps can I take today?**
  Invest in myself and my career so I can serve my family and my clients. BE love.

Step-by-tenuous step, I took the path laid out before me. I found the courage to speak up and set clear boundaries about what I would let into my life. Life shifted dramatically when I declared: "I will no longer settle, especially in my primary relationships. I'm worth it!"

I also wrote a short outline, "Calling in My Love" which included:

- We are healthy in mind, body, *and* spirit.
- We feel safe—mentally, physically, and financially.
- We play in and on the water.

Imagine my surprise, when a few months later, I met a kind, generous, and healthy man online who owned a large sailboat! We quickly fell in love and are sailing along the coast of California on our forty-six-foot sailboat as I write this. Soon, we will be married.

I wasn't looking for a husband, per se; I was looking for a partner, and I welcomed this next stage by being my own best friend.

With a growing sense of safety, I began to trust myself again and lean into my intuitive abilities and knowing. I learned to tell the truth—even when it isn't convenient. When I hear that familiar voice that asks, "Am I too much?"; "Not nice?" or, worse, "Am I being selfish?" I acknowledge it, but don't allow it to stop me from boldly expressing my truth.

Today, I rarely second guess myself, because I ask for what I need and share what works for me, *and* what doesn't. I'm not afraid to share my imperfections, in fact they are what make me "real."

I now know that my goal is not to be perfect, but to love deeply. My job is to let my love shine through. My challenges are the grit that continue to polish the lens of my life so I can see clearly what's true and right for me and my family. I use the guideposts of love, connection, trust, and partnership to navigate my life.

I've become gentler with myself, even when I'm sad, mad or frustrated. I tell myself "Life is a process and *everything*, even the difficulties, are here to help us learn, grow, and prosper." Life is a creative journey to be savored, and not a sprint to check the boxes. Struggle is a necessary part of our evolution.

Being fully expressed isn't always the easiest path, but it makes for deeper, more authentic relationships. Asking for what I need gives others permission to do the same.

I can honestly say that I love my life! I choose how I spend my time, and with whom I work. I love transforming lives, as I work with women who struggle with the burden of doubt, fear, and confusion as they navigate big changes. I can relate to their need to come back to themselves, as they recover from over-care and over-giving.

Life shifts quickly when we make ourselves a priority and fill our love-cup full-to-overflowing. We become our own best champion when we align with our most cherished values and honor our non-negotiables. As we turn a new chapter, we try out new ways of being and *see what works for us*. We rely less on what society tells us is right and lean into what we know to be true for us. We trust ourselves again as we re-write our internal dialogue and see ourselves as heroines, rather than victims, of our lives.

When we slow down enough to dance to *our own drum beat,* we hear the inner voice that says, "You are loved! All of you is welcome." When we pause to listen, our bodies give us abundant information. These messages guide us to heal and prosper.

I know I was sent here to be a channel for those who yearn to ignite their courage and embrace their inner strength, joy, and "juicy aliveness." And, through it all I continue to pray, "Show me!"

ABOUT THE AUTHOR: Carrie Asuncion, MA offers intuitive insight to women, helping them to trust themselves as they navigate BIG CHANGES. With a unique blend of feet-on-the-ground common sense and magic, she quickly transforms self-doubt and confusion to confidence and courage as they boldly take steps to live a life they love. Over a decade ago, Carrie retired from her position as a VP of Human Resources to follow her passion for Energy Psychology. Since then, she has helped thousands of heart-centered women ditch stress and reclaim their joy. When she's not coaching and leading transformational retreats, she enjoys biking, walking the beach, hiking in the redwoods, and sailing along the Central Coast of California.

Carrie Asuncion, MA
Speaker, Transformational Life Coach
KeysToEmpowerment.com
Carrie@KeysToEmpowerment.com
805-305-9255

CHAPTER 13

Forgiveness

Julie King

"Empty your cup so that it may be filled;
become devoid to gain totality."
~ *Bruce Lee*

The burning fragrance of nag champa takes me back to Thailand. To 2011, when at the age of twenty-nine I shot a music video with an Oscar-winning film director Waleed Moursi for my single "Forgiveness" in Phuket. It felt as if I had transcended into a parallel Universe. The locations were breathtaking. One scene was shot inside a magnificent temple. With my production crew and sixteen-millimeter film camera, we walked up the stairs. As we entered the temple we were astonished by its glorious architecture—a large hall with tall ceilings supported by marble pillars, opened-wide windows, and giant gold Buddha statutes embedded with rare size gemstones. The shrine was covered with flower arrangements, hundreds of burning candles, and the potent scent of sandalwood incense soaked through our clothing. Although we were given consent to shoot the video inside the temple, I sensed the need to ask for permission directly from the monks. I wanted to honor their sacred place of chants and mantra meditations. With the help of my translator I spoke to the lead monk, who replied that it was not his approval I needed to seek. "Ask Buddha," he said, and pointed to the shrine. Everyone got silent.

I turned and walked over to the shrine and kneeled in front of Buddha's statue. I put my hands in a prayer position, bowed down, and closed my eyes. I prayed to Buddha, asking for his blessing and that he guide me and help me spread the importance of the message in my song. I believed that it would help millions of people find forgiveness in their hearts. Suddenly everyone gasped, and when I opened my eyes I saw a yellow butterfly circling around me. It flew above my head and over the shrine, then landed right on top of the bouquet of yellow flowers that were placed in front of the statue. With a smile on his face, the monk came up to me and helped me to my feet, as the translator told me that I had Buddha's permission. The butterfly remained in the same place until Waleed said, "That's a wrap."

My association with the metamorphosis of a caterpillar to a cocoon, and then into a butterfly, stayed with me for many years. This moment made me reflect on the message of forgiveness that I was conveying to my audience, and I had a revelation. There was someone I still had to forgive, and ironically it was someone to whom I had dedicated the song. Even though I wrote the song about it, I still hadn't fully gone through the process myself. I felt like a hypocrite, but at the time I wasn't ready to forgive because my childhood wounds were my source of creativity.

Forgiveness was the pivotal point of healing my inner child and the key to my spiritual awakening. I became aware of the need to heal when, at the age of twenty-five, I found myself on the bathroom floor with blood flowing down my face after my engagement party. I remember running across the field away from my ex, barefoot, half-naked, and thinking to myself, *I want to live, I am strong enough to leave, I will make it.* A few days later I was sitting in the office of a psychiatrist who asked me a series of questions that triggered past memories I had buried deep within. My ex was sentenced to jail time, but I knew that it was the resentment for my father that I needed to let go of. I felt resistance, even as I tried every method available. The imprint of physical, verbal, mental, and spiritual abuse had groomed me to tolerate abusive men and toxic relationships.

The tolerance for the emotional pain was high, and as I walked on eggshells, I allowed men to walk all over me. I was caught up in a vicious cycle.

I didn't speak to my father for twenty years, ten years of which he wrote me letters I didn't open. I was engulfed by my own shadow, feeding on it for inspiration and causing more suffering to myself. It wasn't until the age of thirty-four that I was ready to face my demons.

My father babied me until the second day of grade school. As I was doing my first math homework assignment he hit me over the head until blood came out of my nose. I was terrible in math and the truth is it never quite settled in my brain. My father wasn't a drunk, or a drug user. He was a math teacher with a PhD, a sober man, making conscious choice to use violence. He would use the way people were treated under the communist regime to justify his actions. He was ashamed of me. I spent most of my childhood running away from home to my grandmother's, watching my older sister getting abused, covering up bruises on my body, and lying about it to my teachers. I spent hours hiding, praying to God on the cold tile bathroom floor, asking Him to take me. I saw plenty of hospitals where casts were plastered on my wrists, elbows, and shoulders. My father called me weak, and said that's why my limbs would dislocate, not because of him pulling my arms out of the sockets. We were poor, and when in the third grade I lost a red beret hat my father was furious; he beat me with an umbrella that dented the fronts of my legs. (Come to think of it, I don't own any red hats to this day and I just turned forty.) My mom divorced him when I turned thirteen and she, my sister, and I moved from Kazakhstan, Almaty to Santa-Maria, California. My last words to my dad were, "I hate you, I swear you will never see me again."

For me, forgiveness took place during a vision I had at a *Clarity Breathwork™* retreat in Mt. Shasta, shortly after my thirty-fourth birthday. On my eight-hour drive from Los Angeles, I remembered my mom giving me my first conscious breathwork sessions when I was seventeen. During my first breathe, I was numb, my body was frozen. I don't remember having any changes or experiencing any visions. There was no emotion, just numbness, and when Mom asked what was coming up for me, I would reply that I didn't feel anything and all I saw was darkness. Now that I am a facilitator, I know that it was from the state of shock that my body was in, and from stuffing down my feelings. If I showed any emotions during the beating, my father hit me harder.

Then, at the retreat at Mt. Shasta, something incredible happened. The following is an excerpt from my journal, dated August 14, 2016.

Today, during my morning meditation a Goddess handed me a butterfly. It gives me a sense of strength, security, and hope that I am being guided. This is a sign that I am on the right path. I think I was a caterpillar who crawled and crawled. Right now I know I'm in the cocoon, waiting for my transformation to take place. Before I fill myself with something new, I must empty that which I have been holding onto for decades. It no longer serves me.

Intention: Must let go of fears and let go of pain. Must face my shadow, and befriend my demons.

I am ready!

***

During the breathe I experienced something phenomenal. I channeled an incredible vision, and my Universe exploded. I felt different. Everything had shifted. As I got into the rhythm of my breath and tapped into my subconsciousness, all I could see was darkness. Then, I heard a voice of a child crying out for help. My heart clenched in my chest. I walked towards the voice. When I came close I saw a boy, and when our eyes met in his gaze I recognized my dad. I picked him up in my arms and said, "Don't be scared, don't cry, you are

*not alone, I am here." An overwhelming feeling of love came
over me, then there was a bright flash and a wave of emotions
came up to the surface. My heart chakra popped as my heart
cracked wide open. My body jolted and began vibrating. The
feelings of humility, tenderness, compassion, and forgiveness
poured over me and through every cell of my body like a warm
stream of water. It felt as if I was elevating above the floor.*

On that day my kundalini opened.

When the session ended I sent a text to my sister asking her for
our dad's information. She was shocked. When I dialed the number
he didn't answer, and didn't pick up for three days. This feeling I
felt was foreign to me because it was the first time in my life that I
was worried for my father's well-being. A lot of thoughts crossed
my mind. I hoped that he was alive so I could tell him that I for-
gave him. When he finally picked up the phone, I asked him not
to speak, just listen. I shared with him my experience during my
session and on the other side of the line I heard my father sobbing.
With a tremble in his voice he said, "You described one of my
nightmares except for one detail: I was about five years old, alone
in the dark. I was scared, crying, and calling out for Mom. Out of
nowhere, a woman appeared. She picked me up in her arms, told
me not to cry, that there is nothing to fear. She started to sing a song
and a bright flash above our heads revealed a beautiful temple with
yellow butterflies everywhere."

That night we spoke on the phone for hours, both crying, and
healing each other.

Once I came home to Los Angeles, during my integration, I
went into my closet and pulled out an old shoe box where I kept
Dad's letters. As I opened each one at a time, a different type of
healing was moving through me—understanding. In the letters my
father shared the abuse he endured from his mother. My dad was
starved, beaten, placed on his knees in the corner for hours by my

grandmother, bless her soul. His father, may he rest in peace, was locked up for many years in a mental institution. At the end of each letter he added, "P.S. Daughter, please forgive me. I love you, Papa."

My experience made me realize how powerful and profound breath medicine is. I had an epiphany: that *time* is infinite for the soul, and *time* can be bend as we are all connected through one source, the unconditional love of the Universal Being—and that through self-healing it is possible to heal the ancestral tree fourteen generations backward and forward.

My dad had his own healing journey and plenty to forgive himself. It took us four years to find common ground. Three years to finally get to the place for me feeling confident and strong enough to facilitate breathwork for him online. Twenty-seven years to feel safe to see him in person. This summer, eight years after that healing in Mt. Shasta, I am traveling to Prague for our reunion.

"Forgiveness" was selected for *Grammy* nominations in several categories. The song played on ten thousand radio stations around the world. MTV streamed the music video in twenty-five countries. We won twenty-four awards, including best music video, best female leading role, best film director in the *Las Vegas Film Festival* and *Chicago Film Festival*; we also received rave reviews in *The Hollywood Reporter* and over two million views on YouTube. Also, hundreds of thousands of people came forward and shared their stories of forgiveness with me. Shortly after, I retired from the entertainment business and became a breathwork facilitator and sound healer to be in service of humanity. I now lead workshops in Bali, Thailand, Turkey, Sweden, Mexico and throughout the US. I spoke at the *Breath Festival* in Mexico, *Rebirthing Summit, Breathe for Life* at the Life University in Sweden, and on *Awake TV* with Kathleen Riley. I released a three-week meditation program that is based on seven chakras, with specific frequencies congruent with each chakra, its related organs and energy auric fields, in combination with conscious breathing and *Shintao-Shamanic* healing sounds. I became an author and published *Facilitators Workbook*.

One of the greatest gifts one can give themselves is forgiveness. To sing of forgiveness or to say "I forgive you" does not mean that forgiveness has taken place in our hearts. To forgive, one must be ready to let go. To be forgiven, one must have the patience for the other to forgive. Forgiveness can only come from the space of unconditional love and it is one form of self-healing and self-love. Through forgiveness I began living in alignment with my true authentic self.

"Now I wonder: Am I a man who dreamt of being a butterfly, or am I a butterfly dreaming that I am a man?" ~ Buddha

ABOUT THE AUTHOR: Julie King is an internationally acclaimed musician, professional member of Academy of the Grammy, International Breathwork Foundation, Global Practitioner Breathwork Alliance, and International Reiki Center Association. She is the founder of Breathwork Miracles™, developer of multidisciplinary program Trans Breath™, and author of *Facilitator's Handbook*. Julie holds MFA and BFA degrees from California Institute of the Arts in Opera Vocal performance, music composition and production. She is a Certified Clarity Breathwork practitioner, Master Teacher Usui and Karuna Reiki Holy Fire III, life coach, hypnotherapist, and an active Vedic psychologist. Julie resides in Miami and facilitates in person and online workshops.

Julie King
Breath Works Miracles
breathworksmiracles.com
breathworksmiracles@gmail.com

CHAPTER 14

Surrendering Control to Resurrect My Soul

Corissa L. Stepp

I t was a hot, balmy day, and as I quietly pulled out of the driveway and headed to the airport, I knew that something deep within me was simmering beneath the surface. I just couldn't put my finger on it. Arriving at the airport, nothing eventful occurred, and it wasn't until I was seated on the plane, cruising thirty thousand feet above the earth, that I started to feel the onset of a panic attack.

It wasn't the first. That had happened about ten years earlier, also on an airplane. I guess you could say I did not like NOT being in control, and flying is indeed a stark reminder that you are NOT in control. You are at the mercy of the aircraft and, hopefully, adept pilots at the helm. Surrendering to forces outside myself was not something I was entirely at peace with.

Thankfully, I had recently learned how to stimulate my parasympathetic nervous system through a breathing technique, and used it to breathe through the panic attack, regrounding myself mid-flight. As my nervous system calmed, I suddenly realized that I'd spent most of my life trying to control everything around me. I realized all the trauma that I'd survived, from working in Lower Manhattan on 9/11, to being home alone during a home invasion a month later, to watching my father die from the excruciating pain of pancreatic cancer, all before I turned twenty-six, left me with PTSD.

I, the queen of preparation, hated uncertainty and felt extremely uncomfortable when the world around me felt out of control. If things were beyond my control, then that meant I couldn't know what to expect next which left me anxiety-ridden. Yet, here I was, on a plane, going to visit a friend whose world had been rocked in the most unimaginable way possible and nothing was in her control.

Two years prior, Alicia had been diagnosed with triple-negative breast cancer weeks after her fortieth birthday. Then just months after she was deemed "in remission," she was diagnosed with metastatic breast cancer. To say that the rug had been pulled out from under her is an understatement. Alicia had two young children under the age of three and a supportive, loving family who were left reeling after her MBC diagnosis. She looked frailer than the last time I had seen her only months before, yet she still had the same vibrancy and upbeat personality.

One afternoon, Alicia and I were sitting outside in the shade chatting when she asked me a question I wasn't expecting: "Who do you think will be the first to get divorced out of our group of friends?"

Her question wasn't as surprising as the answer that flew out of my mouth: "You mean outside of Joe and me? I'm not sure."

If Alicia was shocked, she didn't reveal it. She just earnestly asked, "Do you really think you'll get divorced one day?"

I put my head down, stared contemplatively at the leaves rustling on the trees, and felt my heart sink into the ground.

Immediately, I realized what had been lurking beneath the surface earlier that morning and in the weeks leading up to it—I was deeply unhappy, maybe even depressed. I felt stuck. This realization would launch me deep into a self-discovery journey to remember who I once was, and figure out how I had become so lost.

Watching Alicia interact with her family, seeing how deeply connected she and her husband were, and knowing that it might all potentially get cut short with her recent diagnosis, caused me to question why it wasn't me in her shoes. I had become a zombie, going through the motions with no clear direction or purpose. My life didn't feel meaningful in any way or to anyone except maybe my children.

Nineteen years earlier, I'd had everything going for me. I was living in New York City, in great health, making good money working in finance at a prestigious investment bank. My job was mentally stimulating and challenging, and I felt fulfilled for a few years, but eventually, I felt like something was missing.

I'd always had a deep desire to help others, but struggled to figure out how I could use my skills to do that in a career. This struggle would continue for nearly ten years until I got married and had kids.

Becoming a mother was life-changing and felt deeply fulfilling. I redefined what success meant to me. My value was no longer defined by the paycheck and bonuses I pulled in; it was in whether or not my child was happy, eating, sleeping, and hitting all his milestones ahead of schedule. I was proud, and I felt gratified. That lasted through the birth of our second son; however, after he turned two, that familiar nagging feeling that my life was lacking meaning and direction appeared again.

It wasn't until that conversation with Alicia, nine years after my first child was born, that I realized I had become a hollowed-out version of myself, to the point that I had become unrecognizable. A storm started brewing inside me; I knew that if I didn't figure out what was "wrong with me," I might run out of time without ever having fulfilled my purpose, dreams, or desires.

Sadly, Alicia passed later that year, and even as I brokenheartedly watched her light dim, I realized she had lit a fire within my soul to seek and find my purpose. I needed my life to have meaning so that when my time came I too could pass with the ease, grace, and gratitude Alicia had embodied throughout her life.

I needed to begin LIVING my life for ME, rather than trying to meet the expectations of everyone else. I'd spent years as a serial people-pleaser, and as a result I had completely lost myself.

Desperately seeking answers, I booked a session with an intuitive. I figured I had nothing to lose—if she ended up being a phony, at least I would be entertained for an hour and have a good story to tell. The session, however, blew my mind. She seemed to know things about me that I was scared to admit to anyone else. Her reading validated and confirmed many things I knew to be true or explained exactly how I felt and what I had experienced.

At the end, she told me that my guides insisted I look into this "thing called Human Design," something she admitted she knew nothing about. *Hmmm*, I thought, *that's weird*. She also told me I was highly intuitive and that my guides have been communicating with me, that I needed to trust it, and that they wanted me to learn how to strengthen my abilities because leaning into my inner guidance would serve me well in this next phase.

After the session I immediately launched the web browser on my phone and typed "Human Design" into the Google search bar. Little did I know I was about to jump head-first into a rabbit hole.

Human Design is a synthesis of five ancient wisdoms and quantum physics. It is a brilliant self-discovery tool that helped me rediscover who I am, reframe my flaws as my natural talents and gifts, and find my purpose.

As I dove deeper and deeper into my self-healing journey, I learned how to connect with and trust my Intuition, which was a big deal for someone who wasn't comfortable trusting or surrendering to the unknown. I also became an EFT practitioner, an energy psychology modality known as "tapping."

Relying on these healing modalities allowed me to slowly zoom out on my experiences and see with greater and greater clarity how my thought and behavior patterns impacted what I'd created throughout my life, and how my perspective was filtered through the lens of the conditioning field I was surrounded by.

By transforming my story from one of victimhood to empowerment, I was able to take accountability for my role in creating it. I had been contorting myself into a pretzel trying to fit into the box other people had placed me in. Through Human Design and tapping, I finally began to see the light at the end of the tunnel. I could choose something different, a different ending! I could rewrite my narrative and become who I wanted to be, not who everyone else told me to be.

This allowed me to experience freedom in a way I never had before. I could finally step into my power, use my voice and ask for what I needed. While I enjoyed nurturing and providing for my loved ones, I also realized how I often felt bitter, overwhelmed, and frustrated when I overcommitted myself because it would leave me with little time or energy to do the things that were fulfilling and meaningful to me. Understanding my Human Design gave me the biggest permission slip to be my authentic self, to follow MY joy, and to set clear and healthy boundaries. It helped me REMEMBER who I am—the person I had lost so long ago. Human Design provided me with a roadmap to reach my highest potential.

There were no shortcuts; I had to go deep into the shadows, wrestle my demons, and come out on the other side. Through tapping, I rewrote my self-limiting beliefs, identified my toxic codependent tendencies, and healed the wounds of my inner child.

Self-healing is an ongoing process; we are all at different points along our journey, searching for the truth of who we are. The world is constantly conditioning us, and our most significant wounds may come up in different ways, often through our relationships. I've learned not to lose faith or hope when this happens. The Universe only brings us what we can handle, and each time old wounds resurface, it is to bring up another piece of the puzzle that needs to be healed, reframed, or brought into alignment.

When we can continually commit to doing the work by staying

curious and aware of who we are and who we are not, understand and cultivate our natural gifts, and come into communion with our faith and intuition, the path before us becomes illuminated.

That afternoon sitting outside with Alicia, I felt like I was asleep at the wheel of a vehicle I didn't recognize, and when I woke up, I was about to slam headfirst into a wall. After awakening and removing the foggy distortion of my conditioned perception, I handed over the keys to my Soul, and now, my Heart is the roadmap I am following.

I spent years trying to find all the answers by thinking through the challenges life threw at me. However, I have since learned to get out of my Head and into my Heart so I can allow Divine guidance to lead me forward. When I spend too much time in my head, I feel incredibly anxious from all the pressure to "figure it out." The minute anxiety creeps into my awareness, frustration usually follows, and then comes fear and doubt. I fear that I won't get it right or perfect, that I may repeat a mistake of the past, or that I will fail, be rejected, or not know enough to move forward. Fear kept me stuck for so long; to be honest, it is what keeps us stuck from living our lives in alignment.

The only way to move past the fear is through love. Learning to love myself and trust the Universe was how I moved forward. Once I could quiet my inner self-critic and accept myself for who I was—the good, the bad, and the ugly—I could begin loving myself again.

Shifting my mindset from focusing on the negative to intentionally grounding myself in the positive altered my trajectory. Being grateful for all of my past experiences, regretting none of them, and learning the lessons helped me step out of victimhood and into empowerment.

I could not become who I am until I experienced, understood, and remembered who I was not. I never would have found myself had

I not first been lost. I never would have reconnected to my purpose had I not first been disconnected. I never would have experienced living my life in alignment had I not first been so grossly out of alignment. I'm now a recovering control freak, perfectionist, and people pleaser, and if I could learn how to surrender to something bigger than myself and be guided back to my Truth, Joy, and Purpose, then so can you!

ABOUT THE AUTHOR: Corissa is a Relationship and Human Design Coach. She graduated from James Madison University with a degree in Quantitative Finance and Financial Economics. She began her career on Wall Street, working for various prestigious Investment Firms. After experiencing a significant life disruption, she embarked on a journey of healing and self-discovery and became a Quantum Human Design™ Specialist, Life Coach, and EFT Practitioner. She now helps clients release thought and behavioral patterns that are holding them back, allowing them to step into a more empowered, authentic, confident, and interdependent version of themselves so they can create, rebuild, or attract meaningful relationships that align with their true value and worth.

Corissa L. Stepp
Relationship and Human Design Coach
corissastepp.com
corissa@corissastepp.com
917-740-6402

CHAPTER 15

Answers in Unexpected Places

Shannon N. Smith

I felt anxious as I sat in the doctor's office. I don't know the exact words he said but it was something like, "The diagnosis is confirmed and you'll be taking pills for the rest of your life. Don't change anything, we'll figure out the right dosage, and you'll be fine." A few weeks prior, I'd received a tentative diagnosis of myasthenia gravis. I was shocked at the quickness and ease of the first appointment. After two years of my body "giving up on me," it took five minutes and a few manipulations for the doctor to say, "I'm pretty sure this is what you have but I'd like some tests to confirm." Early the next morning I went to the lab to have blood drawn and was then off to the airport for an African adventure.

I look back on that 2012 trip, from the diagnosis, to excitement, to the James Bond-like experience that followed—and wonder how I made it the full two weeks. I realize the perspective I had to gain about myself as a result of my body "changing." I see the awareness I needed, the blind hope, and the people who were (and weren't) there to help me when I couldn't help myself. I look back on what I endured because I thought I had to. It was a microcosm of my entire life—of everything that had to be unwound to get to a point where I could see past a diagnosis.

I'll never forget the nurse's face when she told me they'd have to test my facial muscles for the EMG. She didn't know the doctor had already told me they would test my entire body—calves, quads, biceps, and cheeks. I wasn't prepared for that needle, but I don't know how I could be. She placed the electrodes on my face, then sat close holding my hand as the machine turned on over and over and tears rolled down my face. Ten years later, I'm still grateful for her because I felt so alone in that moment. I was strong but I didn't want to be.

That had always been my role: Hold it together. Have the answers. Figure things out. Don't let them see any weakness. Do what it takes to get the job done. But what happens when you don't have the strength? You lie and make up excuses. You push through the day, go home, and cry. Rinse and repeat. You hope "it" will get better because you're actually feeling worse than before.

I developed a hyper-awareness of my body and environment. The things you have to pay attention to with medication, food, rest, and surroundings would surprise you. You never forget the first time you fall down a flight of stairs or the first victory of carrying something up a flight unassisted. I think about those days and laugh at how the Universe works: I had to learn to slow down, listen to my body, and work with it. I had to be aware of sleep, medication dosages, and how my body reacted differently to certain pills depending on the manufacturer's formula. I had to let my pride go and advocate for myself at times. My body wanted a voice and alignment, and I had no choice but to oblige and change as its needs did.

I find it perfect that all the things I had to learn are things I help people with now. Get more order in your life, remember your worth, connect to your body, and ask questions about what feels good. These are all things that I've had to unwind, including all the beliefs, emotions, energetics, and lifetimes that go on with it. To seek answers, because they come eventually.

I'm still trying to figure out how I stumbled upon energy healing. I remember hearing about Reiki, researching, and finding myself in a session with a sound bowl on my stomach feeling underwhelmed and waiting for something to happen. Two days later I burst into tears and cried for days after that. It scared me because I wasn't "a crier," and embarrassing because I didn't want to be perceived as weak. Now I know it was the beginning of my body releasing years of holding everything in. A few months later, when I said yes to Reiki training, I met someone, for the first time, who'd healed themselves without medical intervention. This was the invitation I needed and the possibility I was waiting for. After years of looking in the mirror wondering if I'd wake up normal again, it suddenly stopped seeming impossible.

Pandora's box was open. All of the years of holding my tongue, not having an opinion, being afraid of emotions, living for others... it was all starting to surface. Was I ready? No. Was it time? Yes. I experienced a bad healing crisis because of my body's release and discovered essential oils. Though I didn't quite understand what happened, I was sold!

The more I was willing to try something new, another layer would reveal. And the more I addressed layers as they came up, the more I discovered how much had been hidden. So many wants, dreams, and desires weren't mine, but I carried them as my creation. That's a hard pill to swallow, you know? Realizing you've built up a life that is filled with everyone except you. What do you like? What makes you happy? What are you good at? I thought I could answer for myself, but I really couldn't.

In 2018, when I was asked, "Why are you holding onto the diagnosis?" for the second time, I finally listened. I'd dismissed it the first time because I was offended (actually, it was more like infuriated and "How dare she say that?"). The coach said my guides were asking, that they wanted to know, but how rude! And why would I hold onto something like that?! It didn't make sense. But when a mentor asked the same question a few months later, I couldn't deny it. I still couldn't fully receive the question either, but I was fed up with years of being in victim mode, of taking pills, and feeling frustrated and helpless. That day, I officially started the journey to break free from medication and, four years later, I'm glad I did. I found mentors and classes that provided me with tools and helped me understand and release. I learned that we carry things in multiple layers of our being and that all must be addressed to fully heal. I also learned that *I* am a powerful healer. I learned that energy and science make a good team. I started to believe in magic!

The body is the ultimate machine, and I'd always known I'd do something working with it. Growing up, I was an athlete and fascinated with sports medicine. I even liked getting injured because I enjoyed the physical therapy process and the therapists were nice. I wanted to be an orthopedic surgeon for a sports team, until I found Kinesiology and athletic training in college. They were the perfect mix of working with the body and fun. But it wasn't in the cards. I had the opportunity to work in South Africa for a summer—one I couldn't pass up—and that sent me down a completely different path.

Long but necessary, that path—a sixteen-year detour in management consulting—helped me discover a new world, how to be successful there, and a new version of me. It's amazing how we can become really good at something and make a career of it, but it can be so wrong for our soul.

The desire to do something with the body never waned. In the background, I dreamed of owning my own business and helping others with their health. I got fitness certifications because I'd need them "one day." But I had a career to develop, an industry to learn, and more education to obtain to be competitive. I discovered new inner grit and determination by putting myself through grad school while working full-time. I got really good at some things at work and then known for them. I experienced some unfortunate treatment early on, but learned a lot. I never quite fit in.

I think back to fighting for my promotions at work and realized there was always a question looming in the background (was I on the right path?), and a disconnect between what I and others wanted. I fought to have what I thought was an equal opportunity as others, but the number of things I needed to heal from an energetic perspective to get to that point...I couldn't begin to tell you. I distinctly remember wondering what I was fighting for. I had conversations with people about the criteria to meet the next level. But for what? The more I examined the more I didn't know and the less clear it got about the position and title. Rather, it became clearer that alignment was calling and I had to answer.

Why do you walk away from a successful career with a great company? Why do you suddenly look at your life and start to evaluate what feels or looks good or right? Why do you say "enough is enough" and finally choose your health and well-being above all? Alignment. I got glimpses of this amazing feeling through healing and energy work and I wanted more of it. So I resigned, prioritizing me for the first time, so I could serve as an example to myself and others of what is possible.

There is a perpetuation by society that we should look, act, and live a certain way and if we don't then something is wrong with us. This happens with our bodies. If they aren't acting a certain way, there's a problem with the body. Notice that. It's a problem with the body, not the environment. In my experience, our bodies and environment have an interconnectedness that is undeniable. Think of the Hermetic phrase "As above, so below...as within, so without." I like to think about the second part relating to our bodies and the entangled relationship they have with our environment.

Our bodies pay the price when we're in stressful jobs, relationships in which we aren't safe to express, when we consume content that doesn't support the balance we crave. I had to be willing to listen and admit that my conscious mind/ego didn't have all the answers and needed to step aside, which was hard. I was also willing to let the versions of me with answers step forward because I knew what

I was doing wasn't working.

I had to cultivate a relationship with my body. I was in my body, but wasn't putting it first. That's one of my lessons because I had to listen when it said rest, or else. Have you ever pushed yourself to exhaustion? I have, and it's not good. When our systems are out of balance, our body will tell us—the question is whether we listen. And with that comes learning to follow and trust our intuition. As someone who operated by needing control, this was new territory. I gave myself permission to ask questions and not force answers or actions.

For a long time I didn't believe answers were possible, so now I love questions and the process of unfolding that comes after. I didn't always believe I was worth having answers, love or health, or anything like that. I was really good at letting others define what I could have and being okay with it. I found myself in the discovery of energy work. I learned how to let my natural curiosity blossom and follow what felt good in a new way. I learned how to connect to others and myself in new ways. I allowed myself to see and be seen in new and different ways, because I am way more than this physical vessel I walk around in. I am worth everything I desired all along.

Ten years ago, when I felt the relief of an autoimmune diagnosis, I was disconnected from my body, unable to identify and express emotions, afraid of everything, and had no sense of self. Now I know how these things contributed to the reality I was living and there were things I had to experience to get to where I am today. These days, when I think about alignment, I think about knowing what my body wants, feeling confident to provide what it needs, feeling good in my skin, a flowing exchange between my internal and external environment and knowing when that's off, and unwavering belief in my intuition and its power to guide me.

I also realize that I've never been alone. Even in the darkest moments there was always support, even if I couldn't see or understand it. I am supported, as we all are, by nature of being here and when we're willing to connect to ourselves and listen to the guidance, we can't ever go wrong.

ABOUT THE AUTHOR: Shannon inspires others to transform their lives by broadening their perspective on wellness. A lifelong lover of the body, Shannon merges concepts from energy work and science to help clients reconnect with their bodies and unlock their magic. Through her own journey with an autoimmune diagnosis, Shannon uncovered the power of energy work, natural solutions, and alchemy in health. She holds a BS in Kinesiology and MBA/ Masters in International Management and the following certifications: ACE (Personal Trainer, Health Coach, Group Fitness Instructor), Reiki Master/Teacher, Access Bars® Practitioner/Facilitator, D-Codes™ Practitioner, Quantum Healing Hypnosis Technique® (QHHT) Level 2.

Shannon N. Smith
SNS Wellness LLC
shannonnsmith.com
hello@shannonnsmith.com
703-283-5459

CHAPTER 16

From Narcissistic Abuse to Alignment of Body, Soul, & Spirit

Paras Moghtader

I am standing on top of the mountainside of Bosque Verde forest in Costa Rica, watching the ocean views. The water is calm and so blue. This is the spot I am building my dream house. I look up and see my life partner speaking to the architects as a massive blue butterfly circles him. He entered my life a few years back and even though we knew each other before that, we quickly became best friends and realized we have the same goals in life.

As I look at the sun shining behind them, I have a moment of realization: *Oh my God, I totally manifested this all those years ago when I used to listen to my Shakti Gwain meditation.* "Envision your safe spot in the Universe," she used to say, and I always envisioned a mountaintop overlooking the ocean, with a big glass and concrete home where I did my yoga on the balcony. It was those years that I did a lot of driving between my yoga studio and the new/old stone home I had bought with my then-fiancé. I used to listen to this meditation over and over again to manifest this safe haven, only to realize it was not coming to fruition...no matter how much I visualized it, it just never happened. Now, here I was, finally on the mountain, though I had arrived via a much different route than I had imagined.

I'd been so sure he was the right one for me when we were at that hipster restaurant in Toronto. His blue eyes, glowing in the dimly-lit place, captured me, his charming and polite offerings touched my heart. I fell hard, and was soon willing to sacrifice anything for him.

In the beginning of our relationship, he was kind, gentle and attentive, and he seemed to completely get what I was all about. He bombarded me with compliments (a technique known as "love bombing," in which an abuser overwhelms a partner with compliments in order to subtly but very quickly gain immense trust so they can then manipulate them). His touch, too, was out of this world; he was actually the one who taught me what affection was. In those early days I felt seen, heard, valued, appreciated, validated, and genuinely loved. But it was more than that—while I had had many nice men interested in me, the attraction had never been mutual. Now I couldn't believe I had found someone who I was "into," and felt like he was into me as well. The intensity was intoxicating; it was only later that I learned another term for this attraction: "Trauma Bond." At the time, I simply believed I had found true, lasting love.

It helped, too, that we shared so many of the same interests, the same fears and insecurities. And, of course, he had a troubling childhood sob story—one that made me want to save him with all this love I had to give.

At the time I was doing really well; I had just moved to Toronto to open my hot yoga studio, which was a dream come true. The studio took off and I was so happy. I had just bought an apartment on the waterfront. It felt great to live the city life once again after living in a small Ontario town for a while.

It is like he knew what I wanted to hear, what I wanted to do, and who I was looking for in a partner. He even did the yoga teacher training and I thought we would make a great team!

Unaware that it was love bombing, I was all in. So when he started telling me what poor taste I had to buy my apartment instead of an old hipster house, I was quick to sell it and move wherever he wanted me to.

Fast forward a couple of years, and my whole life had come crashing down. The man I'd fallen in love with had turned into a monster—someone cold, distant, and cruel.

He would go missing for days and nights on end, always making sure I knew there were other friends, places, and things that deserved his precious attention more than me, and making me feel utterly worthless in the process. And he stopped replying to my texts, too, leaving me panicking about where he was and what I had done wrong.

Of course, I did stand up for myself at first, but every time I tried we'd end up fighting and within a few minutes I would become so confused by his conversation loops that I couldn't even remember what it was all about. I'd find myself profusely apologizing for whatever it was I supposedly had done, begging him not to fight with me or be mad at me. Begging him to go back to being nice again!

These arguments would sometimes carry on all through the night, not only wearing me down emotionally but also intentionally depriving me of sleep. If we weren't fighting, he would achieve the same by keeping me waiting for him all night, knowing I'd be too anxious to go to sleep if he wasn't home. Sleep deprivation is highly detrimental to our mental health and, very quickly, I had no strength and self-belief left. My reality became non-existent.

Then, suddenly, everything would be, not just "fine", but great. And then, back to the love bombing. For example, we took a trip to my home country and he knew exactly where to take me, right down to little romantic nooks and restaurants, motels, and bazars. It would make me forget all about everything that he had put me through before…we would be so happy and in love again, or so I thought. On that trip, I got pregnant. I remembered when we first met, he'd said, "You don't have to be on birth control anymore, we have each other and we will figure it out." I certainly thought that still held, especially since we were now married, but when I gave him the news his eyes turned into lifeless dark circles; he was not happy and made sure I knew that. Have you ever seen the reptilian, lifeless eyes of a narcissist?! You would only know what I am talking about if you have ever been in a relationship with one. It is quite a scary thing to experience. That was the moment I knew that not only was I unsafe, but I was entirely on my own with this baby.

There was much, aside from the drama he caused and I always tried to fix, that was so painful I pushed it from my memory. I do, however, remember the day he nearly pushed me down the stairs while I was two months pregnant. I packed up myself and the dog and spent the next week at my yoga studio. I had no family around at the time.

Once the baby was born (and after the show he put on for everyone to see what a loving husband and new dad he was) and after the midwives left and my family was gone, the sleepless nights and gaslighting began again.

Only this time I couldn't just take it; I had another life to care for. I packed up the baby and went to my parents' house twenty-five hundred miles away. When I got back, he had decided to redo the house; there was no front door (this was winter and it was thirty below out!), no hot water, and no signs of anything being completed.

Boom, just like that, I had become homeless. I asked him to move but he was not going anywhere and we were not safe in that house. I took the baby and rented a house; I also called a lawyer.

My ex's focus was solely on finances; he threatened to take everything away from me; asked me to take his name off of my car; and canceled my credit cards. Thank goodness for good family, good friends, and a great attorney! I managed to rent a lovely place which I later bought (and still own today). It was one of the many gifts the Universe offered me as I was going through such a difficult time.

Don't get me wrong; the red flags were there but I ignored all of them. He ran hot and cold at will, his moods were unpredictable. His actions never matched his words and, while I had never experienced anxiety and depression before, I was now walking on eggshells every minute of every day and crying with my baby in my arms at night. I knew deep down that something was wrong, I could feel it in my gut. But I kept overwriting my intuition and went for it anyway; all I wanted was for him to love me like he had. I'll never forget having this bad taste in my mouth and just ignoring it. My body was trying to tell me something, but I did not know how to listen.

Still, no one outside my inner circle guessed that anything was less than perfect. I showed up for work as if nothing was happening, teaching yoga and managing my studio many hours a week. I looked after my baby, and she and I were inseparable. At the same time, though, I was riddled with severe anxiety and blackouts, and I didn't recognize the person looking back at me in the mirror. I gradually lost my friends, and while that was hard losing myself was even worse. There was a Halloween picture I took of me and the baby and half of my face turned out so dark—it was like a sign. That is when I knew I had to leave.

I had arrived at a crossroads. If I stayed, I would die.

So I left.

Healing is no easy task and requires guidance and persistence. There is also no "one size fits all" approach. Thankfully, I tried a few different methods before finding the one that best suited me.

Here is something I learned that helped me get through, and hopefully will help you as well: Being in a narcissistic relationship does not just happen to you; you are probably a codependent or have traits of codependency. I had to come to terms with mine, accept them, and search for methods that helped rewire my brain.

Once I accepted this, the deep, real work began. I started seeing my codependent patterns and I had to stop myself each time and reflect.

Methods including Hakomi Somatic Psychotherapy, EMDR, my personal yoga and Qigong practices helped rewire my brain. Over time, I was able to address the damage caused and remove the emotional triggers and flashbacks that were causing my anxiety and preventing me from being my true happy, joyful, and positive self. I explored and updated any long-standing patterns, outdated beliefs, and faulty conditioning to ensure it will never happen again. By taking this approach, I was able to finally put my anxiety disorder in the past and move on with my life.

That is how I created the twelve pillars of transformation—literally, each pillar is a step I learnt that helped me come closer to a healed self. These twelve pillars consist of lessons concerning our elemental environment and Ayurvedic practices that relate to our specific Doshas, through the practice of Chöd (this is explained fully in the book Feeding Your Demons: Ancient Wisdom for Resolving Inner Conflict, by Tsultrim Allione), as well as Somatic Psychotherapy teachings on what codependency is and how we could heal from it to attract the right kind of people into our lives.

As we journey through life, we often face challenges that can leave us feeling broken, shattered, and lost. Narcissistic abuse is one of those challenges. It can leave us feeling like we are no longer ourselves—like we have lost our soul, spirit, and sense of self-worth. It was only after I left my ex-husband and started to rebuild my life that I realized how toxic our relationship had been. I had to learn how to love myself again, and it was hard work but was worth it, because I am now happier and healthier, both mentally and physically, than I ever was before. And I am finally able to see myself for who I really am: a strong, capable woman who deserves nothing but the best.

ABOUT THE AUTHOR: Paras Moghtader is a healer who combines mindfulness, Hakomi Somatic therapy, and Ayurvedic techniques to help others heal their bodies and minds and grow into their Dharma (purpose). As a child growing up in war-torn environments, Paras experienced trauma from an early age and learned how to expand beyond its impact to live her life with balance, fulfillment, and ease. Navigating through her own experiences taught her how to take others on their own journeys and develop empowering practices that help them expand past physical, mental, and emotional challenges to feel safe, aligned, and motivated by purpose.

Paras Moghtader
The Vedic Therapist
parasmoghtader.com
contact@parasmoghtader.com
647-985-8012

CHAPTER 17

From Surviving to Thriving

Kim Dowling

Every little girl grows up with dreams for their future. Our imaginations are powerful, and there is so much hope. What did you plan for in your life? What did you dream of as you cast a vision for joy and happiness? I was going to be a wife and a mother, with a loving family full of all good things. That is the dream that carried me into my future.

What I didn't know as a bright-eyed and sheltered twenty-something was that life can be cruel. In the span of seven short years it decided to throw me a few curveballs (actually, it felt more like being run over by a freight train.) First up, two miscarriages and the life-changing news that I was physically unable to have children. From there it was the realization that while my marriage was not bad, we would both be happier if we went our separate ways. That decision made me the first person in my family to get divorced. Divorce dismantles your home and your life and shakes everything up like a snow globe. All we can do is hang on until we get to the other side.

Just as I was starting to get back on my feet, my close-knit family, consisting of a younger brother and two wonderful parents, started moving through crisis after crisis. All of a sudden, I was thrown into a world of critical response and public relations. For two hellish years I woke up each morning thinking, *Well, this can't get any worse*. Guess what? It did get worse—every damn day.

Sure, it's rough when the family you dreamed of creating doesn't materialize; you find your way forward to feel happy again. However, when the family that has always given you safety and love turns toxic, when a parent causes trauma, that creates another level of hurt that I'm not sure any of us are ready for. Every holiday, birthday, family picture, and celebration becomes a trigger and a reminder of what we've lost.

The details are not important; we all have stories. Mine, to endcap the worst decade of my life, was the discovery that my father was not the person I believed him to be. The hurt and destruction he decided to bring to our family felt like the death of the person I loved the most. I felt shocked, disappointed, heartbroken, and completely overwhelmed. My mind and my body were in fight-or-flight mode every minute, but I could not run. I was too busy cleaning up the mess that was left behind in both our personal and business lives.

When you lose your sense of peace and comfort, you can lose sight of who you are. I also lost all trust and safety I carried in this world. My life became a sheer force of will, and I went on the attack, doing everything in my power to hold what remained of our family together, while also trying to protect myself from further disappointment. I wanted to hide and bury the pain, anxiety, depression, and hurt.

What I really did was I buried myself. I had no clarity for what my next steps should be, and though I was busy and successful on the outside I had no light or joy on the inside. I had abandoned myself and everything I dreamed of in life. What was the point? Why work so hard to love when people can disappoint and trick you? Why build a family and life when it can all come crumbling down overnight?

I went out of my way to make sure the friends who loved me didn't see how bad things were, but trauma always finds a way to show through. I had not allowed myself to grieve, and instead was literally eating my feelings away and packing on the weight.

The only thing I could do was to try and create order out of the chaos. To make myself feel like I had some sort of control, I put all my attention on what everyone around me needed, making sure they were happy. I poured my energy and focus into work, and let the care and love I needed slip away. I was making it happen and making it look good, but it was by a thread. I hid my true self away and didn't dare whisper or envision what I needed to heal and dream again.

When you lose what you cherish most in life, it changes who you are as a person. For me, the person I trusted most, showed me he was untrustworthy and deceptive. My father made a mockery of the life we had lived. Suddenly, it was like his children and his wife no longer existed. How do you recover when a bulldozer goes through your world? How do you find the strength?

I discovered it with time.

Let's talk about how to go through surviving some of the worst times of your life, to thriving in some of the best times. With time, I learned that life doesn't get easier, we get stronger. I got better at crushing the obstacles that stood in my way. I had a new empathy and compassion for others with the knowledge that you never know what is going on behind the scenes in someone's world. When I coach and train people today, I can see past what they are saying and I do my best to look for what they actually need to feel loved and supported. Trauma gave me that gift.

One day, when I wasn't looking, God and the Universe brought what I most needed into my life—my now husband. He was a lighthouse along a rocky coastline. Yet it wasn't the perfect love story; in fact, it was a big, balled-up mess. I wanted perfection, God gave me perfect for me, which was love and humor, an extrovert to my introverted nature and, most importantly, the calm to my chaos. When I needed everything to be perfect to feel like I was in control, I was given the person who showed me how good life could be even when it's messy.

I could feel the darkness lifting with the sense that a new chapter was up ahead. The world was different now. I was stronger and ready to stop letting the fear of the unknown control me. I was ready to show up with courage and a new resolve. I had survived and developed a tenacity that did not exist in my life before facing seemingly insurmountable odds.

All of us need someone to remind us how perfectly beautiful and capable we are in this world. My husband gave me that gift. I was carrying so much anger that I wanted to scream, every day. We can't go around screaming at everyone, so I kept pushing that anger down. Laughter and happiness replaced that anger and disappointment. Proof once again that love can break down the strongest walls.

For so long, I had silenced my voice and my dreams. Being able to sit calmly and start to remember that everything is not a crisis gave me a chance to forgive, let go, and start over. No matter how hard the past has been, we have the ability to begin again. We can take a deep breath, pick ourselves up, dust ourselves off, and re-build. It was time to start dreaming again. It was time to wake back up to life.

I have learned how to handle difficult times better. Today there is very little that can shake me to my core, though, to be very honest, there are few people I easily trust. We all have scars, that's one of mine. A blessing I discovered is that when you lose what you value most, you realize what really matters can't be taken away. What really matters is living a life that leans into our full potential.

All will be calm, and all is under control

We each live with a light that we carry within, and to stay in alignment with our dreams we must protect that light. Hurdles and failures may pull us down, but we can use them to make us stronger. We can learn that challenges and obstacles are preparing us for the future. It's ok if you can't see it yet. You will learn to see other things as you hear new whispers in your heart.

You get good at seeing drama and deception.

You get good at solving problems and finding solutions.

You get good at staying calm inside the storm.

You get good at taking risks, knowing you will always survive.

You get good at leading people forward to their best lives.

You get good at facing each day with clarity and clear action.

All of this can be a very uncomfortable place to be. If you falter and take a wrong step, it's okay. If you are still unsure at times and a little bit afraid, it's okay. Allow yourself grace and forgiveness as you build your confidence and belief in yourself. I am still working to shed the past and lean into the future. I am still working on releasing the weight I gained during the most stressful times. I had *literally* weighed myself down to keep myself still—to keep myself from the fear of trying and failing.

As I was building my endurance to reach outside of my comfort zone, still afraid, all I could do was follow my instincts to get back to who I was meant to be. Our greatest journey is to live the life of our dreams, and I had wasted too many years already trying to run from fear and pain. Our dreams don't always look like what we wished for, instead our dreams become true to who we should become. May we honor where we are today and learn to trust the process forward.

Everything that you carry in your heart can come true. Today, as I look around at the life I have rebuilt, I can clearly see the gifts I have been given. Isn't it funny how in the midst of a storm, we cannot see. It is only once the storm passes and we look back that we can sit in gratitude. For me, the storms of life painfully cleared out the people, places, and things that were no longer serving me.

On the days that felt unbearable and heartbreaking, I was building the strength I would need to endure. You have built the same strength in life through your journey. The bigger your future, the stronger you need to become. The impact you are meant to make in this world will equally match the strength the universe will push you to build. For all the betrayals and deceptions along the way, God is clearing your path and opening new doors.

We become fearless women, ready to conquer the world. We learn not to be led by the fears that run through our minds, but to overcome every obstacle. If I could do one thing in this life, it would be to inspire the people around me to be brave and move forward with courage.

Sometimes life is about risking everything to continue forward with the dreams that no one can see but you. It's almost liberating to discover that no one has your fate in their hands, no one can stop you, no one can hold you back—you are powerful beyond measure. All you must do is keep fighting forward one step at a time. Make a promise to yourself that you will disappoint others before you let yourself down for one more day. That's how we find ourselves again.

Give it another chance. Take another risk.

We are all given a crossroads in life where we have a choice to accept the pain and hurt we have endured and allow it to hold us back—or we can decide to risk it all again and reawaken the passions we carry. When it feels like the sky has fallen in on us it takes all our energy and focus just to survive. When the opportunity presents itself, we must allow ourselves to heal and find a way to start again. Rebuild, change direction, new people, new places, new habits, and boundaries…whatever it takes. Being fearless isn't being unafraid, it's being terrified and doing it anyway.

For many years I carried pain, needed more sleep than I could get, and had a hard time pushing through and finding creativity. Today I am prioritizing caring for myself, and grateful for my health and capacity to create the life of my dreams. My story is not pretty, and the details are not easy to discuss. I chose to focus on being the best version of me, and to help as many people as I possibly can. We get to do magical things with our lives, and I am not going to waste that journey. When we choose to pick ourselves up and keep moving forward with courage; that's when we get to grow and thrive.

"Our job is not to deny the story, but to defy the ending—to rise strong, recognize our story, and rumble with the truth until we get to a place where we think, Yes. This is what happened, and I will choose how the story ends."
~ *Brené Brown, Rising Strong*

ABOUT THE AUTHOR: Kim Dowling is a lifelong real estate entrepreneur, marketing and social media strategist, and certified personal and business coach. For over thirty years, Kim has led many high-producing sales teams with hundreds of members and coaching nationwide. After serving clients for decades in Atlanta, Georgia, Kim transitioned her business to the Florida Gulf Coast. She is the founder of Coastal Luxury Partners, a real estate brokerage based in Sarasota, Florida. Kim lives along the Manatee River in Bradenton with her husband Joe. She is on a mission to educate and elevate others through teaching, coaching, and speaking.

Kim Dowling
Author, Coach, Trainer
kimdowling.com
kim@kimdowling.com
941-877-1527

CHAPTER 18

Sailing Lessons
Aligning Toward a Vision
Kathy Sipple

*"The voyage of the best ship is a zigzag line of
a hundred tacks." ~ Ralph Waldo Emerson, Self-Reliance*

First Mate

*"For whatever we lose (like a you or a me),
it's always our self we find in the sea."
~ E.E. Cummings*

S hortly after graduating from the University of Michigan in 1988 I accept my computer programmer boyfriend's proposal of marriage. We both have job offers at the same software development company in Milwaukee, Wisconsin and sign a lease on a charming vintage apartment with a view of Lake Michigan. We take sailing lessons together—how romantic!

The first ripple of trouble begins when our employer files bankruptcy. We scramble to find new jobs while continuing to plan our wedding, a stressful process as it becomes evident that our expectations about the life we are building together are divergent. Our marriage—and sailing—both require a level of cooperation and communication beyond our current capabilities as a team. We separate just before our one-year anniversary and divorce six months later. Initially I am numb and feel like a failure, but through the painful process, flashes of insight let me know it was okay to let go. I begin the journey to myself I had never taken...

Destination Revealed

"Live your life by a compass, not a clock." ~ *Stephen R. Covey*

At the age of twenty-six I am living alone for the first time in my life, and I embrace it as an opportunity to turn my attention inward. I begin to see what a gift it is to reimagine my life on my own terms.

In my new, tiny apartment, I begin to meditate regularly. I meet my Higher Self. She shows me a vision forty or so years from now. My blond hair is now snow white but my blue eyes are recognizable. They sparkle like mine, but they are happier and wiser. She lives in a cooperative of some sort with a diverse group of people she loves and who love her. She is a trusted elder and has somehow been instrumental in bringing about this community perched next to a lake and surrounded by woods. She shares information about natural health and spiritual education with those who live there, as well as occasional visitors who come to learn during their stay. There are many more vivid details and nuances I excitedly capture in my journal upon waking. I lovingly nickname her "The Old Woman of the Woods."

This vision is like a lighthouse beckoning me from a distant shore. Though I don't yet know exactly how I will get there, I now have a destination guiding me. I sense that before recoupling I need to become stronger, more fully myself. I realize I have been too busy concerning myself with others' needs and expectations to reflect upon my own.

I reacquaint myself with my Inner Child. I listen to my body and realize she craves touch, so I schedule regular massages. She also wants to sing, make art, and spend time in nature. I also train my Inner Parent to take a more balanced approach toward her role. She will no longer get to dictate goals, but must take direction from the Inner Child and Higher Self too. I applaud her desire to track the goals in a log, though, as this will be useful feedback to know how we're doing. I reflect often on where I am investing my time and effort—the logbook shows me patterns that lead to personal growth and increased happiness when my actions support and align with my values.

My Higher Self gently nudges me to take a yoga class offered at my gym. It is new for me to slow down—previously I had gravitated toward aerobics classes or kickboxing. When I observed people doing yoga it was hard to see how they were *doing* anything. Once I experienced it myself though, I learned the value a gifted yoga instructor adds to the process. Sometimes I thought I was doing a pose correctly but a few gentle adjustments from the instructor made all the difference. Besides the benefits to my physical and spiritual health yoga offered, I also met some wonderful friends in my class. These new connections opened new pathways of learning to me including herbalism, tarot, Reiki, *A Course in Miracles,* and Kabbalah. I begin to trust my body's wisdom to guide me where I need to learn and grow.

My Adult Self is our Captain. She becomes skillful at integrating all the players with day-to-day requirements while not losing sight of Higher Self's long-term vision. She follows career opportunities that hold the most promise for growth and learning. She becomes a top-performing sales professional and then a sales manager. She builds up her retirement savings. She knows that having "enough" money is not the end goal but will put enough wind in her sails to make better choices in alignment with her purpose. She buys a house on her own, close to family but far away from any lakes where she can sail. All the while, her little blue sailboat waits patiently on a trailer in the driveway, for its next adventure.

By age thirty-one I am ready to love—and sail—again.

Setting Sail

"On a day when the wind is perfect, the sail just needs to open and the world is full of beauty." ~ Rumi

One June evening, after a four-hour drive, I am greeted by a gorgeous view of my beloved Lake Michigan in Michigan's Harbor Country. I have arrived early for a wedding rehearsal dinner and am enjoying a glass of wine on the restaurant's terrace. Aside from the bride and groom I don't know anyone very well. My loose plan is to go to the wedding the following day then continue on to Milwaukee and Chicago and spend the rest of the week visiting friends I haven't seen in a long time.

As I sip my wine, I realize weddings no longer trigger me. I am simply a guest, not a "divorced woman with a failed marriage." I look up when a tall man approaches and asks if he may join my table. His name is John. He has driven from Chicago and is also early for the same rehearsal dinner. Over more wine, we share details about ourselves. The conversation flows easily. We continue talking after the rehearsal dinner and arrange to meet in the morning for breakfast before the wedding. We sit next to one another at the wedding too.

He is also taking the week ahead as vacation and has invited a houseful of friends and family to join him for the upcoming Fourth of July celebration at his lake house in the woods. He invites me to join them and I accept, saying I'll be there after I have visited with my own friends. Away from him for a few days, I reconsider, wondering if he had invited me just to be polite; however, a phone call from him to see if I'm still coming convinces me to go.

Our time together is magical; being with him feels like home, like I am somehow more fully myself with him. After a few years of dating long-distance and nightly phone conversations, I move north to Chicago to be with him. It melts my heart when John changes the ball bearings on the boat trailer and tows it himself to the lake house in Michigan for me. Though he is not a sailor, he knows how much I love it. He's a Libra, an air sign, and I'm a Cancer, a water sign—together, we contain the elements to sail metaphorically together! When we marry, we keep the plan just between the two of us. The ceremony takes place in the snowy northern woods with only a minister, a witness, and our Black Labrador retriever.

A Shared Vision

*"I'm not afraid of storms, for I'm learning how
to sail my ship." ~ Louisa May Alcott*

We honeymoon at the same lake house where we first met and invite friends and family to join us to celebrate our marriage after the fact. I remind John about my vision of the Old Woman of the Woods. There are elements of it that feel like what we are experiencing now—togetherness, nature, sharing. Yet it is also different— we are older but also we are not the hosts, paying for everything and making all the decisions alone. Instead the property is owned jointly and responsibilities shared. That part feels important. For now, we enjoy our good fortune and celebrate our new marriage with our guests.

In sailing, if your destination is upwind, it is impossible to sail directly there; instead you need to be able to tack, to shift the rudder and the sail one way and then the next while remaining fixed on an end destination. John and I communicate what we notice—changes in the wind—and decide together how and when to adjust our course. During our twenty-plus years together we navigate a move to a new state, downsizing, losing a business (and, eventually, buying another), bankruptcy, career changes, stock market crashes, health crises, betrayals, and deaths of loved ones.

We work individually and as a couple to become more agile, more resilient in the face of emergencies and now want to help others feel more prepared and connected. John researches how to transition the business he has built into an employee stock ownership program. I start a timebank in which members trade time instead of money. One of the most popular offerings in the timebank is a sailing experience on Lake Michigan! The timebank member who owns the boat meets news friends and enjoys letting everyone take a turn at the helm. He receives maintenance help on the boat in return. It's a first step toward operating cooperatively.

Timebanking leads me to other interesting groups and projects. I join HUMANS (humans united in mutual aid networks). I visit the Venus Project in Florida, a new socioeconomic model utilizing science and technology. I attend Chicago's First Cooperative Economic Summit. I study Michael Tellinger's Ubuntu Movement and Transition Town. I attend Asset-Based Community Development training at DePaul University in Chicago. I attend social permaculture training called Activating Cultural Emergence with Looby Macnamara, Starhawk, and Jon Young in Oakland, California. I feel like a busy bee collecting pollen for the hive, though the hive isn't quite ready to receive it yet. Most people I talk to have a hard time understanding what I'm doing.

The Horizon Nears

"The sooner we learn to be jointly responsible,
the easier the sailing will be." ~ Ella Maillart

It's March 2020 and we are in a global pandemic. I am fifty-three, John almost sixty. Like most of the rest of the world, we are making adjustments to our routine, including our work lives. My in-person marketing training work comes to a halt and I am left with too much time on my hands and missing connection and purpose, as well as a lack of income.

Marketing no longer holds my interest the way it once did, but I have not integrated the new tools I have been learning about into a career—to this point it has been more of a passion project. I update my LinkedIn profile with some verbiage about "resilience" and "regenerative economy," along with some of the things I've been working on. Within weeks, my needed opportunity finds me! Governance Alive in Washington D.C. is starting a training institute (online due to covid-19) and they want marketing help to get them up and running. They will be teaching various social technologies, and will start with "Sociocracy," a term I learn translates to "deciding together."

I love what I learn about sociocracy and their approach, which involves making sure every voice is heard and also checking in with the body's wisdom to determine if a proposal has inner consent. I enroll as a student in the training and immediately begin to use what I am learning to conduct more effective meetings. The teams I have been trying to lead are finally "flocking together" and don't need me to lead them, merely to facilitate. This feels like the missing piece I have needed to activate great ideas into successful projects.

Participants in my courses tend to be conscious evolutionaries, sustainability professionals, blockchain companies, creative types, and some even specifically work with intentional communities! We learn from one another in our monthly study groups. I begin to assist with training the beginner Sociocracy course. I can't get enough of it!

As we near the end of 2022, I am nearing completion of my credentialed program toward becoming a Certified Sociocracy Facilitator and Consultant. Though I am still learning, my new skills have already given me the tools I need to catalyze some big projects focused on climate change. I am meeting more and more people who use sociocracy in intentional communities and cooperatives. By the time I reach that not-so-distant shore of my vision I'm more confident than ever that I will know just what to do!

ABOUT THE AUTHOR: Kathy Sipple is available to help communities build resilience through social technology, climate action, timebanking, and permaculture. She is a certified Sociocracy Facilitator and is working on a book called *Social Climate* expected to be published in 2023. The book will serve as a guide for communities to address environmental and social justice issues while enriching the quality of life. Sipple holds a degree in Economics from the University of Michigan and is a member of Mensa. She lives in Valparaiso, Indiana—the "Vale of Paradise"—with her husband John and their black Lab Bodhi.

Kathy Sipple
CoThrive Community
kathysipple.com
kathy@kathysipple.com
219-405-9482

CHAPTER 19

Who Do You Trust When You're Unique?

Karen Flaherty

"If you are always trying to be normal,
you will never know how amazing you can be,"
~ *Maya Angelou, writer, poet, activist*

I've always been a little weird. I never felt like I fit in; on the other hand, I never really wanted to. But that wasn't very satisfying either. It wasn't until I learned to be aligned through a combination of modalities that I've found inner peace, fulfillment, and an inner knowing that works ALL the time!

Very few people understand me and my quirkiness. Various people—including friends and family—have thrown accusations at me: "How dare you?", "How could you?", "Who do you think you are?" Original, I know. They never accused me of doing anything *to* them, of being disrespectful or harmful; I just wasn't behaving in a way they were expecting. It was based on a previous version of me—the generous, kind, subservient, people-pleasing me. They've also thrown names—bitch and witch are the standouts. The rest I've conveniently filed away.

By the time I found the Law of Attraction in 2000, I had already started taking courses and seminars, reading books and attending conferences about motivation and self-awareness, and taking responsibility for my life and my actions. After studying Abraham-Hicks, *The Secret,* and other teachers of the Law of Attraction for almost ten years, I was introduced to Human Design in 2009. That seemed to be the key to the kingdom. All my questions were answered—over time and to this day. There were lots of confirmations as well. If I was ever in a sticky spot, I always trusted my gut—usually after all the other options had been tried.

Since learning about Human Design—a personality-assessment tool in which I'm now certified—I've run thousands of charts, done hundreds of sessions with my clients, spoken at dozens of holistic fairs, and studied relentlessly to fully understand it. It had to be logical for me. That's who I am—a geek who doesn't trust others to come up with new ways of doing things, unless I can prove they work. And I wasn't going to risk my reputation for something that was considered too "out there" by business associates, friends, and family. (They still think I'm weird, but less than they used to.)

As Ra Uru Hu, the creator of Human Design, says: "There is only one major dilemma in being human. And that dilemma is: 'Can I trust the decisions I make?'"

I should add that before I learned about my Human Design chart and how to make decisions, I was a classic bumbler. In fact, for the first fifty-two years of my life, I *never* trusted my decisions. I always felt like I was flying by the seat of my pants and the sky was about to crash in. I went to school, worked in Corporate America for over thirty years, got married, and did all the things you're supposed to do. I made a lot of decisions.

Now, they weren't all bad decisions—some of them turned out remarkably well, like saying yes to my husband of twenty-nine years. But I never, ever trusted my decisions at the time I was making them. And that's where finding out about the Law of Attraction and Human Design made all the difference. I could stop worrying, stop being a nervous wreck, and stop beating myself up when I made the wrong decision. I even eventually learned how to live in the moment. It was a huge change in my life—and in my peace of mind.

"Be yourself. Let people see the real, imperfect, flawed, quirky, weird, beautiful, and magical person you are." ~ *Unknown*

Finally, I figured it out: My particular brand of weirdness is what makes me unique.

And I have to say: The life I live and love now looks nothing like what I was born into and grew up with for the first fifty years.

Through Human Design, I realized there was more to me than I'd thought—including that I was supposed to be a teacher and a guide for others. Once I had my chart explained, I started to make choices using my decision-making strategy (which is "wait to respond"), choices that felt good, and listened to that little voice (my Inner Being), pointing me in the right direction.

I was finally able to say, "Here's who I am and here's what I want to do with my life." It took a while to get comfortable with that. Moving from Corporate America to having my own business—that was a leap. I did it slowly but surely, with lots of ups and downs. And then I got laid off in the spring of 2014, literally the week before our house went on the market, with all the painters and electricians running around! That was actually good news. It meant that once we settled into our new home in Florida, I could do Human Design full-time. It seemed like a sign from the Universe!

I had lists of intentions for each area of my life, and the Universe provided, and is providing for us, daily. I knew that I wanted to have my own coaching practice one day, and that day is here, now. It's a blessing for me to be able to help my clients find out who they really are and get past their fears, like I did. But I have to tell you that getting past those fears—some from childhood, some acquired later on—took the most time. And I'm still healing physically from some of those fears because they had such detrimental effects. That's why I'm writing about alignment: to give you a framework to think about decision-making and the fears surrounding those decisions; to show you the awareness that's available to you; and to provide some tools to get past the fears in a way that, hopefully, will save you some of the time and effort that I went through.

"What is my life's purpose?" That's the question I get most often from my clients. And I was searching for a long time too. We often talk about life purpose as if it's one absolute thing. What I'm finding for myself and my clients is that it evolves, changes, and morphs over time, if we're in alignment with who we are.

As Serena Williams said in a recent interview for *Vogue*: "I have never liked the word *retirement*. It doesn't feel like a modern word to me. ...Maybe the best word to describe what I'm up to is *evolution*. I'm here to tell you that I'm evolving away from tennis, toward other things that are important to me. A few years ago, I quietly started Serena Ventures, a venture capital firm. Soon after that, I started a family. I want to grow that family."

One of my spiritual teachers has said that the "new kids"—those of the GenZ and millennial generations—are the ones we've been waiting for. It's not a coincidence that there are currently over three billion under thirty on the planet. They are the transformational change agents for our future. These kids come in knowing and living their life purpose, at least according to Human Design. They are also much more open to change and, as we know, change is the only constant. So, yes, it's time to buckle our seat belts. We're in for a rocky ride through 2027, and perhaps beyond.

Not surprisingly, my clients have morphed over the past few years from forty-five to sixty-year-old women to GenZ and millennials of all types. This shift has inspired me to write a book about how these generations can find their life purpose, and understand that it's okay to trust themselves, their Human Design strategies, and the Universe.

Over the past two years (through COVID's arrival on the scene), the "new normal" has been boiling us like proverbial frogs in the pot. First, we went through the fear phase (not knowing what was going on or how to deal with it), and then the self-care phase (pretty much only doing what we needed to do to stay healthy and sane).

Now we're into the next phase, where it's time to put the Peloton and comfort cooking away. Fortunately, many people are ready to jump out of the boiling water, claim their place in this new landscape, and move forward with their future plans. Since we're all unique, each plan is different, but I'm really feeling like the time to start is now. (Hint: so if you're not sure of your purpose, this would be a good time to find it.)

Even though our purpose and plans are different, we are energetically interconnected. The Unity Consciousness that Patricia Cota-Robles, author of *The Coming Era of Peace,* talks about (and that I'm comfortable with) is: "We are all one and Love is all there is." It's a very simple philosophy for moving forward, one that honors both our uniqueness on the human level and the fact that energetically, there is no distinction between us. It's quantum physics at work in the here and now. The singularity has arrived.

At the same time, we're in a period of provocation, with so many of us feeling polarized by the "other." While provocation can be positive, in that it triggers emotions that cause us to act in a way that brings us to our goals and aspirations, it can also make us angry, fearful, intimidated, or scared. We all know the bullies who use this energy to great effect. Some are siblings, some are colleagues/bosses, some are politicians. Some are empowering and help us to move forward more quickly or with more enthusiasm; others keep us in "our place" through lies and oppression.

Obviously, these are very different outcomes from the same provocative energy. One is done with love; the other is done with the opposite. I have thought about this provocative energy. In the words of Hippocrates, "First, do no harm."

What I Now Know

Whether you are provoking or being provoked, be flexible, stay in the present, and make a choice that's based on fairness, a choice that is fair and just for you, for all around you, and for the planet. As much as possible, keep your emotions in check, while also being clear about your boundaries.

Beyond that, I'll say that it just doesn't serve us to become angry or fearful or scared for the future. Our vibration is our key to staying present. Living in the past can be depressing and fear of the future produces anxiety. You don't need either of those. Stay present. Deal with each situation and opportunity as it arises. And if someone you know is provoking you in a way that doesn't feel good, you can smile and stay—or smile and walk away. It's your choice always.

You also have a choice in Human Design: to live up to your full potential using your Strategy, or not. Some people think of that as putting limits on what's possible. I prefer to think of it as being in alignment with what you really want. To me, that's having real abundance in life.

Making decisions that are in alignment with your Strategy invokes that blissful feeling—you know—when you're in the flow and life is good. Those decisions just naturally *feel* better. They're the best for you, and they're right for all aspects of your current reality.

As human beings, we can consciously evolve or not.

When we choose to evolve *and* use our Strategy, we're choosing to stay fully alive, rather than living a conditioned and compromised life. A conditioned life means living your childhood conditioning, and/or in accordance with everyone else's ideas of what you should be doing. The compromised life is one with a lot of "shoulds."

While it's hard to ever fully get *over* the conditioning we experienced as children, it's worth a try. The more you can get away from that conditioning, the more freedom you'll feel. With the fully-alive life, you're in the driver's seat: you know your decision-making strategy; you use it to make all your decisions; and as a result, you feel alive, aware, and engaged most of each day. This kind of freedom allows for the growth and joy that we're supposed to be here for: living our purpose in a way that's congruent with our unique design and that just feels right and juicy!

It's always our choice.

ABOUT THE AUTHOR: Karen Flaherty is a certified Human Design Specialist and the best-selling author of *Getting to Know YOU.* Before finding Human Design in 2009, Karen spent thirty years in marketing, training, and sales positions in New York and New Jersey. She brings this wealth of knowledge of the corporate world, and her own life experience, to her Human Design coaching practice. Karen is passionate about helping her clients discover their purpose and their genius. She works with individuals, couples, and families, as well as businesses and entrepreneurs, to find a new way of reinventing their lives in the twenty-first century.

Karen Flaherty
Living by Human Design
livingbyhumandesign.com
karen@livingbyhumandesign.com
386-693-4263

CHAPTER 20

Thriving by
Embracing My Journey

Jamie Allen Bishop

I died when I was seven years old. It was 1979 and during a month of hospitalization, my appendectomy left my formerly healthy vessel septic, with my organs slowly shutting down. Commonly thought of as an out-of- body experience, I left my human form and took a moment to talk to Jesus.

In fact, Jesus took me on a journey to a stunning location that I still visit when I meditate. It was a wide-open and lush green meadow with a babbling brook running through it; a waterfall rumbled gently in the distance. The glen was surrounded by a comforting forest of trees and brush. There were loads of children and plenty of animals there, too. I felt completely safe and was quite tempted to join the children, some of whom were playing a game I recognized. I had never seen anything like it before and have not seen anything like it since. It is my happy place.

Jesus and I came to rest on an imaginary seat and looked down at my sick little form. He expressed that it was up to me whether I stayed in this body, in this experience, in this lifetime. Or I could come with Him and play with the children in the meadow.

I remember looking down at my toxic body, contemplating my decision. I watched as my mom held my hand. Her exhausted head not quite sleeping on the hospital bed, tear-stained cheeks, slicked back hair, silently praying for me to live. I remember her scrubs (she was in nursing school at the time) and her unrelenting insistence to remain by my side (long before family members were allowed to stay in a hospital room). She went without food for far too many hours each day, and it took every nurse, doctor, and family member to convince her to take a break...to go get some air...to take a shower.

She was breaking.

While I could feel the freedom that staying with Jesus and those children would have brought me, I didn't feel there was any other choice. I chose to stay...to learn...to live.

And that is the decision I come back to whenever I am struggling. I chose this life. Might as well love it, right?

While my near-death experience (NDE) is very important to my story, it is not where my story begins. That beginning occurred in 1975, when my mom and dad lived in a cute little 1929, Spanish-style bungalow in Sunland, California.

As a young couple living on their own for the first time in their lives, they were the epitome of the California dream—a surfer dude with a painting business and a waitress-turned-wallpaper installer, doing what it took to provide for themselves and their two small children.

Little did they know their four-year-old daughter could see and interact with spirits.

One night, while my mom tucked me into bed, I looked over her shoulder, sat straight up and proclaimed, "Mommy, there's a man behind you."

With wide eyes refusing to turn to see where I was looking, and all the little hairs on the back of her neck pricked up to the point of pain, my mom asked me, "Where is he now?"

Innocently and without remorse, I excitedly stated, "He's gone."

I don't remember that experience at all, but my mom recalls the story vividly and is still a little freaked out by it.

Being a sensitive and accommodating child, I quickly learned that talking to my *invisible friends* was "not normal," and that I needed to stop doing it, especially when other people could see me.

With the understanding that I scare people I loved, I gave up my spiritual, God-given gifts to help ease the minds of the adults in my world.

But when it's your calling, it will keep calling.

Those gifts showed up again during my NDE, and then again when I was eighteen years old.

It was now the end of 1989, and my boyfriend and I had been a couple for going on four years. During my first semester of college, we were loving the freedom of being grownups, of making our own plans, of dreaming about the future, and of having fun together. When his father unexpectedly died at fifty-one, it left his family confused, questioning, and hurting. When his dad's spirit appeared to me in the wee hours of the morning as I made my way to the restroom in their family home, I wasn't sure what to do about it.

More than thirty years later, I remember it like it was yesterday. Without speaking or pointing or telepathically communicating words (as ghosts do in the movies), his dad's spirit *energetically* communicated with me. He wanted me to tell his sons and his wife how much he loves them...that they should never question *that*... no matter what else might come into question.

I did. I told them.

The forty weeks that followed this attempt by the Universe to guide me back to my calling were tumultuous (at best)—my parents divorced; my best friend of fifteen years stopped talking to me; my boyfriend was hospitalized for emergency surgery then broke up with me; my mother almost died after ovarian cyst surgery; my younger brother dropped out of high school and came to live with me; our lives were threatened at gunpoint by a neighbor; a restaurant patron (I was a waitress) became a terrifying stalker who threatened my life (*if he couldn't have me, nobody could!*); a coworker was arrested for murdering his girlfriend; my new boyfriend (turns out) was an abusive alcoholic; and I was kicked out of college (*asked to "reevaluate my goals"*).

There is more chaos and mayhem that was not on this list, but you get the gist of what was going on in my life that year. When it comes to suicidal tendencies, I have had my ups and downs throughout this lifetime. If there was ever a time I had reason to *jump this ship* called life, 1990 was it! Looking back, I am absolutely astonished (and grateful) I survived it.

I came back to my decision: *I chose this life.*

Fast forward fourteen years to 2004, when the greatest miracle in the world happened. I became pregnant with the first child I would carry to full term, and while her birth was a struggle for us all, our daughter came into this world with a spirit unlike any other. She is playful, intelligent, beautiful, and wise beyond her years. As a toddler, she looked up at me and said, "I'm so glad I chose you out, mama." (Those words still fill my heart with joy!) I am in awe of her every day. She holds an important piece of my soul forever. My hopes and desires are for her to be the happiest person in the world.

When I was introduced to the spiritual, self-help world of Wayne Dyer, Marianne Williamson, and Deepak Chopra, and so many other personal development gurus in 2005, it felt like I found another missing piece of my soul. The wisdom and grace that surrounded me for the next decade was incredible. Understanding that the experience was not without its trial and tribulations, and there were incredibly trying times, as I look back, I see the growth I achieved, and I am extraordinarily grateful I found that conference and did that personal development work. I followed that conference as a volunteer until 2012. In 2014, we moved across the country creating a new wave of deep growth and spiritual reckoning.

I left that personal growth stuff in the dust to pursue earthly goals—like getting out of debt, buying our first house, working in Corporate America, hobnobbing with the elite, and sending our child to private school.

It was 2017 when I found myself at the edge of the earth—another year where everything seemed to challenge my very existence. I was bullied at work; I was physically sick; my stress levels were insanely high; my environment exposed me to toxic chemicals that wreaked havoc on my lungs; my kiddo was quickly gaining independence, and my life seemed overwhelming and pointless. Suicidal ideations were a real part of my experience—*What if I just speed up around this corner and let my car go over the edge? What if I just take this whole bottle of pills? What if I got into a hot bath and cut my femoral artery? How could I die in a way where my daughter would **not** be the one to find my body?*

Then my daddy died.

I have lost far too many people in my lifetime to death—family and friends, teachers and mentors, colleagues and clients. But there is nothing quite like having your daddy come to you in spirit form.

My daddy—despite his addiction issues, his anger management challenges, and his complete and utter neglect of me (and my brother)—was the apple of my eye. If you asked my mom what I thought of him when I was growing up, she would have told you I thought he walked on water.

And he did.

When he was alive, I could see him for all his potential. I could see *him*...his spirit...his beauty...his love.

After his spirit came to me, I had to release the extreme anger I felt about how much more he was part of my life *after* he died than when he was alive. In doing that release work, I knew why my problems kept coming back to challenge me.

My problem in each of those years where everything seemed to be one extreme event after another was ME. I was sssooo focused on myself, there was no way to see anything else. I was the only common denominator in all my experiences. I became aware that

I was the only one who could view my life in a different way.

I have since realized that to go from being off path to being on path is a matter of perception. I am no longer interested in pursuing a career that doesn't serve my calling, but rather I have become the greatest cheerleader of myself and others to hone their spiritual gifts and share them with the world.

Coping is a funny thing and learning coping mechanisms creates the ability to manage crisis in the moment. These are critical survival skills that are necessary when we are trying to overcome or manage trauma. However, the same coping skills we learn when we are in crisis can also, if we do not do self-healing work, keep us stuck in survival mode for far longer than we need to remain there.

Hindsight being 20/20, I know these experiences and coping mechanisms were necessary for me to have a sense of knowing, to relate to other's struggles, and to be relatable. I know for a fact that when I stopped to examine what my role was in my experiences, I realized how much control I have over this glorious thing called life. I am grateful for each and every moment. As my colleague Cheryl Clark says, "Each moment led me to this." Each story has its own tale to tell, and all of them make me who I am today.

In 2019, my family and I moved back to Southern California where I continue to explore self-evaluation, self-healing, and self-education. I have continued my spiritual journey, which has led me to a beautiful realization. Life is exactly as Florence Scovel Shinn says: "The game of life is a game of boomerangs. Our thoughts, deeds, and words return to us sooner or later with astounding accuracy." The lens through which we view this life makes all the difference in the world.

In 2020, I added Master Life Coach certifications to my more than thirty education certificates. Moreover, I've officially embraced the idea that I am, indeed, a coach. Where a mentor can lead by example and show you what a grand life looks like, and a consultant might evaluate where you're at and create changes that shift things *for* you, a coach is someone who helps YOU figure out who you are, what you want, and why you must pursue it. A coach can guide you from a place of knowing, help you create a plan to get to wherever you wish to be, and cheer you on along your way.

When I think of a world where everyone embraces their gifts and pursues the things that bring them joy, I see a world where love is easy to find, where peace is normal behavior, and where safety is available to all.

When I embraced my own talents, when I chose to be here—to *thrive* while I am lucky enough to live, I became a woman living in alignment, and I want that for every person. My big goal, my vision is to help entrepreneurs all over the globe take those courageous first steps toward embodying their soul's purpose because I know with one hundred percent certainty that when they do, our world becomes heaven on earth.

ABOUT THE AUTHOR: Your magic matters! Embracing your purpose with confidence on social media is what Jamie helps entrepreneurs do. As a Master Life Coach, she lives a legacy life-style she loves—traveling to exotic locations, supporting family members in pursuing their dreams, and bringing peace to the world around her. Through laser coaching sessions, creating a plan of action, and holistic practices, Jamie helps entrepreneurs create thriving lives to bridge the gaps between personal, spiritual, and professional development. You can find her social media accounts by visiting her website at JamieAllenBishop.com

Jamie Allen Bishop
Jamie Allen Bishop, LLC
jamieallenbishop.com
jamie@jamieallenbishop.com
480-203-8911

About the Authors

Are you inspired by the stories in this book?
Let the authors know.

See the contact information at the end of each chapter
and reach out to them.

They'd love to hear from you!

Author Rights & Disclaimer

Each author in this book retains the copyright and all inherent rights to their individual chapter. Their stories are printed herein with each author's permission.

Each author is responsible for the individual opinions expressed through their words. Powerful You! Publishing bears no responsibility for the content of the stories by these authors.

Acknowledgements & Gratitude

To the beautiful authors of this book, we love, respect, and admire you. Your openness with your stories exemplifies your passion for assisting individuals in their lives, and your personal resilience and courage light the way for us to be braver in our own lives. Thank you for sharing this journey with us. We are honored.

Our editor Dana Micheli: Your intuition, sense of humor, creativity, and willingness are a perfect fit to get to the heart of the stories. We appreciate our partnership and friendship, and we love you.

Our training team: AmondaRose Igoe, Kathy Sipple, Karen Flaherty, and Francine Sinclair—your expertise, big hearts, and guidance are so helpful for our authors. We love and appreciate each of you.

Lisa Stamper: We are honored to share this experience with you, and we appreciate your intuitive insights and mission to assist individuals on their personal and spiritual journey.

We are forever grateful for the many beautiful and loving individuals who grace our lives—friends, family, colleagues, our tribe. We're grateful for each of you and for the gifts you generously offer.

Above all, we are grateful for the Divine Spirit that flows through us each day providing continued blessings, lessons, and opportunities for growth, peace, and JOY!

Namaste` and Blessings, Love and Gratitude,
Sue Urda and Kathy Fyler
Publishers

About Sue Urda and Kathy Fyler

Sue and Kathy have been business partners since 1994. They have received many awards and accolades for their businesses over the years and continue to they love the work they do and the people they attract to work with. As publishers, they are honored to help people share their stories, passions, and lessons.

Their mission is to raise the vibration of people and the planet and to connect and empower women in their lives. Their calling has been years in the making 'forever' and is a gift from Spirit.

The strength of their partnership lies in their deep respect, love, and understanding of one another as well as their complementary skills and knowledge. Kathy is a technology enthusiast, web goddess, and freethinker. Sue is an author and speaker with a love of creative undertakings and great conversations. Their honor, love, and admiration for each other are boundless.

Together their energies combine to feed the flames of countless women who are seeking truth, empowerment, joy, peace, and connection with themselves, their own spirits, and other women. They believe we are all here in this lifetime to support and love of one another, and they are grateful to fulfill this purpose through their publishing company.

Connect with Sue and Kathy:

Powerful You! Publishing
powerfulyoupublishing.com
goodvibesgals.com
sueurda.com

About Lisa Stamper

Lisa Stamper is an Intuitive Life and Business Coach, Spiritual Channel, Healer, 2x Best Selling Author, International Speaker, and Founder of many courses and a membership to help people tap into their inner power, deepen their intuition, and connect to their sacred selves so they can live a thriving, rich, freedom filled life in alignment with their soul.

Lisa is a powerful catalyst, activating people's unique soul gifts; helping them step into their life's purpose so they can experience more EASE, FREEDOM, FULFILLMENT, FUN and FLOW in their lives. It is from the deepest truth of her heart and intention to lead with love to serve the greater good; helping humanity to heal, evolve, and ascend so as many people as possible live their lives deeply connected to their inner selves and the wellspring of love and guidance within. She also works with heart centered entrepreneurs to start and grow their businesses using practical and soul inspired strategies to maximize their success.

Lisa teaches and speaks on topics of true success, manifesting, energy, business, wealth, intuition, mindset, purpose, passion, alignment, empowerment and living life from soul. She's shared the stage with Jack Canfield and been a featured speaker at Harvard University and many podcasts, summits, interview series and more.

Be sure to check out her free weekly intuitive readings on her Facebook fan page Lisa Stamper Mind Body Spirit to help you navigate the current energies and align with your highest path.

lisastamper.com
lisastamper@1cloud.com
Instagram: @lisastamperintuitive
Facebook: @lisastampermindbodyspirit
TikTok: @intuitivelisastamper

Powerful You! Publishing
Sharing Wisdom ~ Shining Light

Are You Called to be an Author?

If you're like most people, you may find the prospect of writing a book daunting. Where to begin? How to proceed? No worries! We're here to help.

Whether you choose to contribute to an anthology or write your own book, we're here for you. We'll be your guiding light, professional consultant, and enthusiastic supporter. If you see yourself as an author partnering with a publishing company who has your best interest at heart and expertise to back it up, we'd be honored to be your publisher.

We provide personalized guidance through the writing and editing process, as well as many necessary tools for your success as an author. We offer complete publishing packages and our service is designed for a personal and optimal author experience.

We are committed to helping individuals express their voice and shine their light into the world. Are you ready to start your journey as an author? Do it with Powerful You! Publishing.

Powerful You! Publishing
239-280-0111
powerfulyoupublishing.com

Collaboration Books

Empowering Transformations for Women
Women Living Consciously
Journey to Joy
Pathways to Vibrant Health & Well-Being
Women Living Consciously Book II
Healthy, Abundant, and Wise
Keys to Conscious Business Growth
The Gifts of Grace & Gratitude
Heal Thy Self
Empower Your Life
Heart & Soul
The Beauty of Authenticity
WOKE
The Art and Truth of Transformation for Women
Women Living On Purpose
U Empath You

ALIGNMENT...

It's a Feeling and
A Knowing.

Tap into Your Heart.
Feel it in Your Body.
Live it in Each Moment.

Made in the USA
Middletown, DE
04 November 2022

14127510R00097